Cram101 Textbook Outlines to accompany:

The Cultural Landscape: An Introduction to Human Geography

James M. Rubenstein, 9th Edition

A Content Technologies Inc. publication (c) 2011.

PRACTICE EXAMS.

Get all of the self-teaching practice exams for each chapter of this textbook at
www.Cram101.com and ace the tests. Here is an example:

Chapter 1

The Cultural Landscape: An Introduction to Human Geography
James M. Rubenstein, 9th Edition,
All Material Written and Prepared by Cram101

I WANT A BETTER GRADE.

1 _____ are interdisciplinary fields of research and scholarship pertaining to particular geographical, national/federal, in the practice of scholarship, many heterogeneous fields of research, encompassing both the social sciences and the humanities. Typical _____ programs involve history, political science, sociology, cultural studies, languages, geography, literature, and related disciplines.

○ Area studies   ○ Abandoned village

○ Abatis   ○ Abbas Rizvi

2 _____ is the variety of human societies or cultures in a specific region) There is a general consensus among mainstream anthropologists that humans first emerged in Africa about two million years ago .

○ Cultural diversity   ○ Cabinda

○ Cable-stayed bridge   ○ Cabo da Roca

3 _____ is an interdisciplinary field combining approaches from academic geography with the traditional subject matter of social science, thus emphasizing population issues such as tourism, urbanisation, and so on.

_____ broadly differs from physical geography in that it has a greater focus on studying intangible or abstract patterns surrounding human activity and is more receptive to qualitative research methodologies. It encompasses human, political, cultural, social and economic aspects of the social sciences.

○ Human geography   ○ $H_T O$

○ Habitat   ○ Habitual abortion

You get a 50% discount for the online exams. Go to **Cram101.com**, click Sign Up at the top of the screen, and enter DK73DW5929 in the promo code box on the registration screen. Access to Cram101.com is $4.95 per month, cancel at any time.

With Cram101.com online, you also have access to extensive reference material.

You will nail those essays and papers. Here is an example from a Cram101 Biology text:

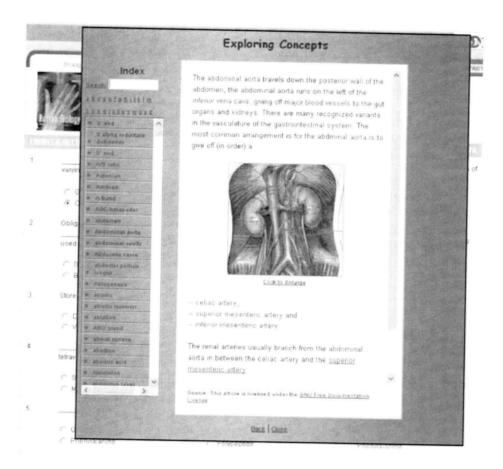

Visit **www.Cram101.com**, click Sign Up at the top of the screen, and enter DK73DW5929 in the promo code box on the registration screen. Access to www.Cram101.com is normally $9.95 per month, but because you have purchased this book, your access fee is only $4.95 per month, cancel at any time. Sign up and stop highlighting textbooks forever.

Learning System

Cram101 Textbook Outlines is a learning system. The notes in this book are the highlights of your textbook, you will never have to highlight a book again.

How to use this book. Take this book to class, it is your notebook for the lecture. The notes and highlights on the left hand side of the pages follow the outline and order of the textbook. All you have to do is follow along while your instructor presents the lecture. Circle the items emphasized in class and add other important information on the right side. With Cram101 Textbook Outlines you'll spend less time writing and more time listening. Learning becomes more efficient.

Cram101.com Online

Increase your studying efficiency by using Cram101.com's practice tests and online reference material. It is the perfect complement to Cram101 Textbook Outlines. Use self-teaching matching tests or simulate in-class testing with comprehensive multiple choice tests, or simply use Cram's true and false tests for quick review. Cram101.com even allows you to enter your in-class notes for an integrated studying format combining the textbook notes with your class notes.

Visit **www.Cram101.com**, click Sign Up at the top of the screen, and enter **DK73DW5929** in the promo code box on the registration screen. Access to www.Cram101.com is normally $9.95 per month, but because you have purchased this book, your access fee is only $4.95 per month. Sign up and stop highlighting textbooks forever.

The Cultural Landscape: An Introduction to Human Geography
James M. Rubenstein, 9th

CONTENTS

Area studies	Area studies are interdisciplinary fields of research and scholarship pertaining to particular geographical, national/federal, in the practice of scholarship, many heterogeneous fields of research, encompassing both the social sciences and the humanities. Typical Area studies programs involve history, political science, sociology, cultural studies, languages, geography, literature, and related disciplines.
Cultural diversity	Cultural diversity is the variety of human societies or cultures in a specific region) There is a general consensus among mainstream anthropologists that humans first emerged in Africa about two million years ago .
Human geography	Human geography is an interdisciplinary field combining approaches from academic geography with the traditional subject matter of social science, thus emphasizing population issues such as tourism, urbanisation, and so on. Human geography broadly differs from physical geography in that it has a greater focus on studying intangible or abstract patterns surrounding human activity and is more receptive to qualitative research methodologies. It encompasses human, political, cultural, social and economic aspects of the social sciences.
Country	In geography, a Country is a geographical region. The term is often applied to a political division or the territory of a state, or to a smaller, or former, political division of a geographical region. Usually, but not always, a Country coincides with a sovereign territory and is associated with a state, nation and government.
Developed country	The term Developed country is used to describe countries that have a high level of development according to some criteria. Which criteria, and which countries are classified as being developed, is a contentious issue and there is fierce debate about this. Economic criteria have tended to dominate discussions.
Abraham	Abraham is the founding patriarch of the Israelites, Ishmaelites, Edomite, and the Midianites and kindred peoples, according to the book of Genesis. In the absence of extra-biblical evidence for his existence, influential scholars have long questioned the historicity of his narratives. Judaism, Christianity, and Islam are sometimes referred to as the `Abrahamic religions` because of the progenitor role Abraham plays in their holy books.
Al-Idrisi	Abu Abd Allah Muhammad al-Idrisi al-Qurtubi al-Hasani al-Sabti or simply Al Idrisi was an Andalusian geographer, cartographer, Egyptologist and traveller who lived in Sicily, at the court of King Roger II. Muhammed al-Idrisi was born in the North African city of Ceuta (Sabtah) then belonging to the Almoravid Empire and died in Sicily. Al Idrisi was a descendent of the Idrisid rulers of Morocco, who in turn were descendants of Hasan ibn Ali, the son of Ali and the grandson of the Islamic prophet Muhammad.

al-Idrisi`s education was probably acquired in Andalusia.

Land Ordinance of 1785	The Land Ordinance of 1785 was adopted by the United States Congress on May 20, 1785. Under the Articles of Confederation, Congress did not have the power to raise revenue by direct taxation of the inhabitants of the United States. Therefore, the immediate goal of the ordinance was to raise money through the sale of land in the largely unmapped territory west of the original colonies acquired from Britain at the end of the Revolutionary War. In addition, the act provided for the political organization of these territories.
Remote sensing	Remote sensing is the small or large-scale acquisition of information of an object or phenomenon, by the use of either recording or real-time sensing device(s) that are wireless, or not in physical or intimate contact with the object (such as by way of aircraft, spacecraft, satellite, buoy, or ship). In practice, Remote sensing(MRI), Positron Emission Tomography (PET), X-radiation (X-RAY) and space probes are all examples of Remote sensing. In modern usage, the term generally refers to the use of imaging sensor technologies including: instruments found in aircraft and spacecraft as well as those used in electrophysiology, and is distinct from other imaging-related fields such as medical imaging.
World Heritage Site	A UNESCO World Heritage Site is a site (such as a forest, mountain, lake, desert, monument, building, complex) that is on the list that is maintained by the international World Heritage Programme administered by the UNESCO World Heritage Committee, composed of 21 state parties which are elected by their General Assembly for a four-year term. A World Heritage Site is a place of either cultural or physical significance. The program catalogues, names, and conserves sites of outstanding cultural or natural importance to the common heritage of humanity.
Park	A Park is a protected area, in its natural or semi-natural state or planted, and set aside for human recreation and enjoyment. It may consist of, rocks, soil, water, flora and fauna and grass areas. Wilderness Parks are intact and undeveloped areas used mainly by wild species.
Prime meridian	The Prime Meridian is the meridian (line of longitude) at which the longitude is defined to be 0°. (zero degrees) The Prime Meridian and its opposite the 180th meridian (at 180° longitude), which the International Date Line generally follows, form a great circle that divides the Earth into the Eastern and Western Hemispheres. Unlike the parallels of latitude, which are defined by the rotational axis of the Earth (the poles being 90° and the equator 0°), the Prime Meridian is arbitrary.

Cultural landscape	Cultural landscapes` have been defined by the World Heritage Committee as distinct geographical areas or properties uniquely `..represent[ing] the combined work of nature and of man..` . This concept has been adapted and developed within international heritage arenas (UNESCO) as part of an international effort to reconcile `..one of the most pervasive dualisms in Western thought - that of nature and culture`
	The World Heritage Committee has identified and adopted three categories of Cultural landscape, ranging from (i) those landscapes most deliberately `shaped` by people, through (ii) full range of `combined` works, to (iii) those least evidently `shaped` by people (yet highly valued). The three categories extracted from the Committee`s Operational Guidelines, are as follows:
	(i) `a landscape designed and created intentionally by man`; (ii) an `organically evolved landscape` which may be a `relict (or fossil) landscape` or a `continuing landscape`; (iii) an `associative Cultural landscape` which may be valued because of the `religious, artistic or cultural associations of the natural element`
	The concept of `Cultural landscapes` finds its origins in the European tradition of landscape painting.
International Date Line	The International Date Line is an imaginary line on the surface of the Earth opposite the Prime Meridian where the date changes as one travels east or west across it. Roughly along 180° longitude, with diversions to pass around some territories and island groups, it mostly corresponds to the time zone boundary separating −12 and +12 hours Coordinated Universal Time (UTC) (Greenwich Mean Time - GMT). Crossing the International Date Line travelling east results in a day or 24 hours being subtracted, and crossing west results in a day being added.
Ethnic	An ethnic group is a group of humans whose members identify with each other, through a common heritage that is real or assumed. This shared heritage may be based upon putative common ancestry, history, kinship, religion, language, shared territory, nationality or physical appearance. Members of an ethnic group are conscious of belonging to an ethnic group; moreover ethnic identity is further marked by the recognition from others of a group`s distinctiveness.
Functional Region	A Functional region, also known as a Nodal region, is a region that has a defined core that retains a specific characteristic that diminishes outwards. To be considered a Functional region, at least one form of spatial interaction must occur between the center and all other parts of the region.
	A Functional region is under the umbrella of `Regions` one of the five themes of geography the other themes include place, human-environment interactions, location, and movement.

Regional integration	Regional integration is a process in which states enter into a regional agreement in order to enhance regional cooperation through regional institutions and rules. Its objectives could range from economic to political although it has become a political economy initiative where commercial purposes are the means to achieve broader socio-political and security objectives. Past efforts at Regional integration have often focused on removing barriers to free trade in the region, increasing the free movement of people, labour, goods, and capital across national borders, reducing the possibility of regional armed conflict (for example, through Confidence and Security-Building Measures), and adopting cohesive regional stances on policy issues, such as the environment, climate change and migration.
Cultural ecology	Cultural ecology studies the relationship between a given society and its natural environment, the life-forms and ecosystems that support its lifeways. This may be carried out diachronically (examining entities that existed in different epochs), or synchronically (examining a present system and its components). The central argument is that the natural environment, in small scale or subsistence societies dependent in part upon it - is a major contributor to social organization and other human institutions.
Environmental determinism	Environmental determinism, also known as climatic determinism or geographical determinism, is the view that the physical environment, rather than social conditions, determines culture. Those who believe this view say that humans are strictly defined by stimulus-response (environment-behavior) and cannot deviate.
	The fundamental argument of the environmental determinists was that aspects of physical geography, particularly climate, influenced the psychological mind-set of individuals, which in turn defined the behaviour and culture of the society that those individuals formed.
Soil	Soil formation, is the combined effect of physical, chemical, biological, and anthropogenic processes on Soil parent material. Soil genesis involves processes that develop layers or horizons in the Soil profile. These processes involve additions, losses, transformations and translocations of material that compose the Soil.
Everglades	Everglades is also the name of a city in Collier County, Florida.
	The Everglades are subtropical wetlands located in the southern portion of the U.S. state of Florida, comprising the southern half of a large watershed. The system begins near Orlando with the Kissimmee River, which discharges into the vast but shallow Lake Okeechobee.
Diffusion	`Diffusion` is a time-dependent process , constituted by random motion of given entities and causing the statistical distribution of these entities to spread in space. The concept of Diffusion is tied to notion of mass transport, driven by a concentration gradient.
	The concept of Diffusion emerged in the physical sciences.

Taliban	The Taliban is a Sunni Islamist political movement that governed Afghanistan from 1996 until they were overthrown in late 2001 during Operation Enduring Freedom. It has regrouped since 2004 and revived as a strong insurgency movement governing at the local level and fighting a guerrilla war against the governments of Afghanistan, Pakistan, and the NATO-led International Security Assistance Force (ISAF). The movement is made up of members belonging to different ethnic Pashtun tribes, along with a number of volunteers from nearby Islamic countries such as Uzbeks, Tajiks, Chechens, Arabs, Punjabis and others.
Population	IV class="thumb tright"> Distribution of world Population in 1994. Time taken for each billion people to be added to the world`s Population (including future estimates).
Population density	Population density (in agriculture standing stock and standing crop) is a measurement of population per unit area or unit volume. It is frequently applied to living organisms, and particularly to humans. It is a key geographic term.
Folk	The English word folk is derived from a Germanic noun *fulka meaning `people` or `army` (i.e. a crowd as opposed to `a people` in a more abstract sense of clan or tribe). The English word folk has cognates in most of the other Germanic languages. folk may be a Germanic root that is unique to the Germanic languages, although Latin vulgus, `the common people`, has been suggested as a possible cognate.
Demographic	Demographics data are the characteristics of a population as used in government, marketing or opinion research). Commonly-used Demographics include sex, race, age, income, disabilities, mobility (in terms of travel time to work or number of vehicles available), educational attainment, home ownership, employment status, and even location.
AID	Aid is a voluntary transfer of resources from one country to another, given at least partly with the objective of benefiting the recipient country. It may have other functions as well: it may be given as a signal of diplomatic approval, or to strengthen a military ally, to reward a government for behaviour desired by the donor, to extend the donor`s cultural influence, to provide infrastructure needed by the donor for resource extraction from the recipient country, or to gain other kinds of commercial access. Humanitarianism and altruism are, nevertheless, significant motivations for the giving of Aid.

Overpopulation	Overpopulation is a condition where an organism`s numbers exceed the carrying capacity of its habitat. In common parlance, the term usually refers to the relationship between the human population and its environment, the Earth. Overpopulation does not depend only on the size or density of the population, but on the ratio of population to available sustainable resources.
Population growth	Population growth is the change in population over time, and can be quantified as the change in the number of individuals in a population using `per unit time` for measurement. The term Population growth can technically refer to any species, but almost always refers to humans, and it is often used informally for the more specific demographic term Population growth rate , and is often used to refer specifically to the growth of the population of the world. Simple models of Population growth include the Malthusian Growth Model and the logistic model.
Population	IV class="thumb tright"> Distribution of world Population in 1994. Time taken for each billion people to be added to the world`s Population (including future estimates).
Diffusion	`Diffusion` is a time-dependent process , constituted by random motion of given entities and causing the statistical distribution of these entities to spread in space. The concept of Diffusion is tied to notion of mass transport, driven by a concentration gradient. The concept of Diffusion emerged in the physical sciences.
Buddhism	Buddhism is a religion and philosophy encompassing a variety of traditions, beliefs and practices, largely based on teachings attributed to Siddhartha Gautama, commonly known as the Buddha . Buddha lived and taught in the northeastern Indian subcontinent sometime between the 6th and 4th centuries BCE. He is recognized by adherents as an awakened teacher who shared his insights to help sentient beings end suffering, achieve nirvana, and escape what is seen as a cycle of suffering and rebirth. Two major branches of Buddhism are recognized: Theravada and Mahayana (`The Great Vehicle`).
Borneo	Borneo is the third largest island in the world and is located at the centre of Maritime Southeast Asia. Indonesians refer to the entire island as Kalimantan. Malaysians usually refer to the island by the names of either of its two Malaysian states, Sarawak and Sabah.

Ecumene	Ecumene a term originally used in the Greco-Roman world to refer to the inhabited earth (or at least the known part of it). The term derives from the Greek oἰκουμένη , short for oἰκουμένη γᾶ† `inhabited world`. In modern connotations it refers either to the projection of a united Christian Church or to world civilizations.
Guinea	Guinea, officially Republic of Guinea , is a country in West Africa formerly known as French Guinea . The country`s current population is estimated at 10,211,437 (CIA 2008 estimate). Guinea`s size is almost 246,000 square kilometres (94,981 sq mi).
Indonesia	The Republic of Indonesia is a country in Southeast Asia and Oceania. Indonesia comprises 17,508 islands. With a population of around 230 million people, it is the world`s fourth most populous country, with the world`s largest population of Muslims.
Korea	Korea (Korean: i•œêµ or i¡°ì„) is a civilization and formerly unified nation currently divided into two states. Located on the Korean Peninsula, it borders China to the northwest, Russia to the northeast, and is separated from Japan to the east by the Korea Strait. Korea was united until 1948; at that time it was split into South Korea and North Korea.
South Asia	South Asia is the southern region of the Asian continent, which comprises the sub-Himalayan countries and, for some authorities , also includes the adjoining countries on the west and the east. Topographically, it is dominated by the Indian Plate, which rises above sea level as the Indian subcontinent south of the Himalayas and the Hindu Kush. South Asia is surrounded by Western Asia, Central Asia, Eastern Asia, Southeastern Asia and the Indian ocean.
Southeast Asia	Southeast Asia or Southeastern Asia is a subregion of Asia, consisting of the countries that are geographically south of China and Taiwan, east of India and north of Australia. The region lies on the intersection of geological plates, with heavy seismic and volcanic activity. Southeast Asia consists of two geographic regions: the Asian mainland (aka.
International trade	International trade is exchange of capital, goods, and services across international borders or territories. It refers to exports of goods and services by a firm to a foreign-based buyer (importer) In most countries, it represents a significant share of gross domestic product (GDP). While international trade has been present throughout much of history , its economic, social, and political importance has been on the rise in recent centuries.
Population density	Population density (in agriculture standing stock and standing crop) is a measurement of population per unit area or unit volume. It is frequently applied to living organisms, and particularly to humans. It is a key geographic term.

Arable land	In geography, Arable land is an agricultural term, meaning land that can be used for growing crops. It is distinct from cultivated land and includes jungles that are not currently used for human purposes. Arable land covers an area of approximately 12 million square miles .
Crude birth rate	Crude birth rate is the nativity or childbirths per 1,000 people per year. According to the United Nations` World Population Prospects: The 2008 Revision Population Database, Crude birth rate(births in a period / population of person-years over that period). According to the Dictionary of Geography by Audrey Clark, Crude birth rate is also known as natural increase.
Demographic	Demographics data are the characteristics of a population as used in government, marketing or opinion research). Commonly-used Demographics include sex, race, age, income, disabilities, mobility (in terms of travel time to work or number of vehicles available), educational attainment, home ownership, employment status, and even location.
Demographic transition	The Demographic transition model (DTM) is a model used to represent the process of explaining the transformation of countries from high birth rates and high death rates to low birth rates and low death rates as part of the economic development of a country from a pre-industrial to an industrialized economy. It is based on an interpretation begun in 1929 by the American demographer Warren Thompson of prior observed changes, or transitions, in birth and death rates in industrialized societies over the past two hundred years. Most developed countries are beyond stage three of the model; the majority of developing countries are in stage 2 or stage 3. The model was based on the changes seen in Europe so these countries follow the DTM relatively well.
Latin America	Latin America is a region of the Americas where Romance languages - particularly Spanish, Portuguese, and variably French - are primarily spoken. Latin America has an area of approximately 21,069,501 km^2 , almost 3.9% of the Earth`s surface or 14.1% of its land surface area. As of 2008, its population was estimated at more than 569 million.
Middle East	The Middle East is a region that encompasses southwestern Asia and Egypt. In some contexts, the term has recently been expanded in usage to sometimes include Pakistan and Afghanistan, the Caucacus, and North Africa. It`s often used as a synonym for Near East, in opposition to Far East. The corresponding adjective is Middle-Eastern and the derived noun is Middle-Easterner.
Bermuda Triangle	The Bermuda Triangle, also known as the Devil`s Triangle, is a region in the western part of the North Atlantic Ocean in which a number of aircraft and surface vessels are alleged to have mysteriously disappeared in a manner that cannot be explained by human error, piracy, equipment failure, a suspension of the laws of physics, or activity by extraterrestrial beings.

A substantial body of documentation reveals, however, that a significant portion of the allegedly mysterious incidents have been inaccurately reported or embellished by later authors, and numerous official agencies have stated that the number and nature of disappearances in the region is similar to any other area of ocean.

Folk	The English word folk is derived from a Germanic noun *fulka meaning `people` or `army` (i.e. a crowd as opposed to `a people` in a more abstract sense of clan or tribe). The English word folk has cognates in most of the other Germanic languages. folk may be a Germanic root that is unique to the Germanic languages, although Latin vulgus, `the common people`, has been suggested as a possible cognate.
Fertility	Fertility is the natural capability of giving life. As a measure, `Fertility rate` is the number of children born per couple, person or population. This is different from fecundity, which is defined as the potential for reproduction (influenced by gamete production, fertilisation and carrying a pregnancy to term).
Total fertility rate	The Total fertility rate (Total fertility rate period Total fertility rate (PTFR) or total period fertility rate (TPFR)) of a population is the average number of children that would be born to a woman over her lifetime if (1) she were to experience the exact current age-specific fertility rates (ASFRs) through her lifetime, and (2) she were to survive from birth through the end of her reproductive life. It is obtained by summing the single-year age-specific rates at a given time. The Total fertility rate is a synthetic rate, not based on the fertility of any real group of women, since this would involve waiting until they had completed childbearing.
Area studies	Area studies are interdisciplinary fields of research and scholarship pertaining to particular geographical, national/federal, in the practice of scholarship, many heterogeneous fields of research, encompassing both the social sciences and the humanities. Typical Area studies programs involve history, political science, sociology, cultural studies, languages, geography, literature, and related disciplines.
Cultural diversity	Cultural diversity is the variety of human societies or cultures in a specific region) There is a general consensus among mainstream anthropologists that humans first emerged in Africa about two million years ago .
Ethnic	An ethnic group is a group of humans whose members identify with each other, through a common heritage that is real or assumed. This shared heritage may be based upon putative common ancestry, history, kinship, religion, language, shared territory, nationality or physical appearance. Members of an ethnic group are conscious of belonging to an ethnic group; moreover ethnic identity is further marked by the recognition from others of a group`s distinctiveness.

Africa	Africa is the world`s second-largest and second most-populous continent, after Asia. At about 30.2 million km² (11.7 million sq mi) including adjacent islands, it covers 6% of the Earth`s total surface area and 20.4% of the total land area. With a billion people in 61 territories, it accounts for about 14.72% of the World`s human population.
Life expectancy	Life expectancy is the expected (in the statistical sense) number of years of life remaining at a given age. It is denoted by e_x, which means the average number of subsequent years of life for someone now aged x, according to a particular mortality experience. (In technical literature, this symbol means the average number of complete years of life remaining, ie excluding fractions of a year.
Zero population growth	Zero population growthis a condition of demographic balance where the number of people in a specified population neither grows nor declines, considered as a social aim. zero population growth is the ideal to which countries and the whole world should aspire, according to some, in the interests of accomplishing long-term environmental sustainability. A loosely defined goal of zero population growth was to have a fertility rate of 2.11. Fertility rate is the average number of children a woman would be expected to have over the course of her life.
Dependency ratio	In economics and geography the Dependency ratio is an age-population ratio of those typically not in the labor force (the dependent part) and those typically in the labor force (the productive part). In published international statistics, the dependent part usually includes those under the age of 15 and over the age of 64. The productive part makes up the population in between, ages 15 - 64. It is normally expressed as a percentage. This gives: $$(Total)\ Dependency\ ratio = \frac{(number\ of\ people\ aged\ 0\ to\ 14)\ +\ (number\ of\ people\ aged\ 65\ and\ over)}{number\ of\ people\ aged\ 15 \rightarrow 64} \times 100$$ This ratio is important because as it increases, there may be an increased cost on the productive part of the population to maintain the upbringing and pensions of the economically dependent.
Population pyramid	A Population pyramid is a graphical illustration that shows the distribution of various age groups in a population (typically that of a country or region of the world), which normally forms the shape of a pyramid. It typically consists of two back-to-back bar graphs, with the population plotted on the X-axis and age on the Y-axis, one showing the number of males and one showing females in a particular population in five-year age groups (also called cohorts). Males are conventionally shown on the left and females on the right, and they may be measured by raw number or as a percentage of the total population.
Sex ratio	Sex ratio is the ratio of males to females in a population. The primary Sex ratio is the ratio at the time of conception, secondary Sex ratio is the ratio at time of birth, and tertiary Sex ratio is the ratio of mature organisms.

The human Sex ratio is of particular interest to anthropologists and demographers.

Family planning

Family planning is the planning of when to have children, and the use of birth control and other techniques to implement such plans. Other techniques commonly used include sexuality education, prevention and management of sexually transmitted infections, pre-conception counseling and management, and infertility management.

Family planning is sometimes used as a synonym for the use of birth control, though it often includes more.

World population

The World population is the total number of living humans on Earth at a given time. As of 18 November 2009, the Earth's population is estimated by the United States Census Bureau to be 6.798 billion. The World population has been growing continuously since the end of the Black Death around 1400. The fastest rates of World population growth (above 1.8%) were seen briefly during the 1950s then for a longer period during the 1960s and 1970s .

The

The word the is the only definite article in the English language, and the most frequently used word in English the article the is often used as the very first part of a noun phrase in English.

Country

In geography, a Country is a geographical region. The term is often applied to a political division or the territory of a state, or to a smaller, or former, political division of a geographical region. Usually, but not always, a Country coincides with a sovereign territory and is associated with a state, nation and government.

Developed country

The term Developed country is used to describe countries that have a high level of development according to some criteria. Which criteria, and which countries are classified as being developed, is a contentious issue and there is fierce debate about this. Economic criteria have tended to dominate discussions.

Abortion

Abortion is the termination of a pregnancy by the removal or expulsion from the uterus of a fetus or embryo, resulting in or caused by its death. An Abortion can occur spontaneously due to complications during pregnancy or can be induced, in humans and other species. In the context of human pregnancies, an Abortion induced to preserve the health of the gravida (pregnant female) is termed a therapeutic Abortion, while an Abortion induced for any other reason is termed an elective Abortion.

AID

Aid is a voluntary transfer of resources from one country to another, given at least partly with the objective of benefiting the recipient country. It may have other functions as well: it may be given as a signal of diplomatic approval, or to strengthen a military ally, to reward a government for behaviour desired by the donor, to extend the donor's cultural influence, to provide infrastructure needed by the donor for resource extraction from the recipient country, or to gain other kinds of commercial access. Humanitarianism and altruism are, nevertheless, significant motivations for the giving of Aid.

Black Death	The Black Death was one of the deadliest pandemics in human history, peaking in Europe between 1348 and 1350. It is widely thought to have been an outbreak of bubonic plague caused by the bacterium Yersinia pestis, but this view has recently been challenged. Usually thought to have started in Central Asia, it had reached the Crimea by 1346. From there, probably carried by fleas residing on the black rats that were regular passengers on merchant ships, it spread throughout the Mediterranean and Europe. The Black Death is estimated to have killed 30% to 60% of Europe's population, reducing the world's population from an estimated 450 million to between 350 and 375 million in 1400. This has been seen as creating a series of religious, social and economic upheavals which had profound effects on the course of European history.
Cholera	Cholera is an infectious gastroenteritis caused by enterotoxin-producing strains of the bacterium Vibrio Cholerae. Transmission to humans occurs through eating food or drinking water contaminated with Vibrio Cholerae from other Cholera patients. The major reservoir f was long assumed to be humans themselves, but considerable evidence exists that aquatic environments can serve as reservoirs of the bacteria.
Epidemiology	Epidemiology is the study of factors affecting the health and illness of populations, and serves as the foundation and logic of interventions made in the interest of public health and preventive medicine. It is considered a cornerstone methodology of public health research, and is highly regarded in evidence-based medicine for identifying risk factors for disease and determining optimal treatment approaches to clinical practice. In the study of communicable and non-communicable diseases, the work of epidemiologists ranges from outbreak investigation to study design, data collection and analysis including the development of statistical models to test hypotheses and the documentation of results for submission to peer-reviewed journals.
Avian flu	Avian influenza, sometimes Avian flu, and commonly bird flu, refers to `influenza caused by viruses adapted to birds.` Of the greatest concern is highly pathogenic avian influenza (HPAI). `Bird flu` is a phrase similar to `swine flu,` `dog flu,` `horse flu,` or `human flu` in that it refers to an illness caused by any of many different strains of influenza viruses that have adapted to a specific host. All known viruses that cause influenza in birds belong to the species influenza A virus.
Indira Priyadarshini Gandhi	Indira Priyadarshini Gandhi (Hindi: à¤‡à¤‚à¤¦à¿à¤°à¤¾ à¤ªà¥□à¤°à¿à¤¯à¤¦à¤° à¥□à¤¶à¿à¤¨à¥€ à¤—à¤¾à¤‚à¤§à¥€ IndirÄ□ PriyadarÅ›inÄ GÄ□ndhÄ«; née: Nehru; (19 November 1917 - 31 October 1984) was the prime minister of the Republic of India for three consecutive terms from 1966 to 1977 and for a fourth term from 1980 until her assassination in 1984, a total of fifteen years. She was India's first, and to date only, female prime minister. Gandhi was partly educated in India and then in Britain: at Badminton School, a girls` independent school in Bristol, and at Somerville College at the University of Oxford.

Diffusion	`Diffusion` is a time-dependent process , constituted by random motion of given entities and causing the statistical distribution of these entities to spread in space. The concept of Diffusion is tied to notion of mass transport, driven by a concentration gradient. The concept of Diffusion emerged in the physical sciences.
Emigration	Emigration is the act of leaving one`s native country or region to settle in another. It is the same as immigration but from the perspective of the country of origin. Human movement before the establishment of political boundaries or within one state, is termed migration.
Immigration	Immigration is the arrival of new individuals into a habitat or population. It is a biological concept and is important in population ecology, differentiated from emigration and migration. The International Organization for Migration or(I.O.M) said there are more than 200 million migrants around the world today.
Latin America	Latin America is a region of the Americas where Romance languages - particularly Spanish, Portuguese, and variably French - are primarily spoken. Latin America has an area of approximately 21,069,501 km^2 , almost 3.9% of the Earth`s surface or 14.1% of its land surface area. As of 2008, its population was estimated at more than 569 million.
Area studies	Area studies are interdisciplinary fields of research and scholarship pertaining to particular geographical, national/federal, in the practice of scholarship, many heterogeneous fields of research, encompassing both the social sciences and the humanities. Typical Area studies programs involve history, political science, sociology, cultural studies, languages, geography, literature, and related disciplines.
Forced migration	Forced migration refers to the coerced movement of a person or persons away from their home or home region. It often connotes violent coercion, and is used interchangeably with the terms `displacement` or forced displacement. A specific form of Forced migration is population transfer, which is a coherent policy to move unwanted persons, perhaps as an attempt at `ethnic cleansing`.
Ireland	Ireland ; Ulster Scots: Airlann, Latin: Hibernia) is the third-largest island in Europe and the twentieth-largest island in the world. It lies to the north-west of continental Europe and is surrounded by hundreds of islands and islets. To the east of Ireland, separated by the Irish Sea, is the island of Great Britain.
Slavery	Slavery is a form of forced labour in which people are considered to be the property of others. Slaves can be held against their will from the time of their capture, purchase or birth, and deprived of the right to leave, to refuse to work, or to receive compensation (such as wages).

With around 27 million people, there are more slaves in the world today than at any point in history, more than twice as many as all the African slaves brought to the Americas.

Refugee	Under the United Nations Convention Relating to the Status of Refugees from 1951, a Refugee is a person who , owing to a well-founded fear of being persecuted on account of race, religion, nationality, membership of a particular social group, is outside the country of their nationality, and is unable to or, owing to such fear, is unwilling to avail him/herself of the protection of that country.

The concept of a Refugee was expanded by the Convention's 1967 Protocol and by regional conventions in Africa and Latin America to include persons who had fled war or other violence in their home country.

Refugees(UNHCR), which counted 8,400,000 Refugees worldwide at the beginning of 2006. This was the lowest number since 1980. The major exception is the 4,600,000 Palestinian Refugees under the authority of the United Nations Relief and Works Agency for Palestine Refugees in the Near East (UNRWA), who are the only group to be granted Refugee status to the descendants of Refugees according to the above definition. |
| Drought | A drought is an extended period of months or years when a region notes a deficiency in its water supply. Generally, this occurs when a region receives consistently below average precipitation. It can have a substantial impact on the ecosystem and agriculture of the affected region. |
| Floodplain | A Floodplain is flat or nearly flat land adjacent to a stream or river that experiences occasional or periodic flooding. It includes the floodway, which consists of the stream channel and adjacent areas that carry flood flows, and the flood fringe, which are areas covered by the flood, but which do not experience a strong current.

Flood plains are made by a meander eroding sideways as it goes downstream. |
| International migration | International migration occurs when persons cross state boundaries and stay in the host state for some minimum length of time.Migration occurs for many reasons. Many people leave their home countries in order to look for economic opportunities in another country. Others migrate to be with family members who have migrated or because of political conditions in their countries. |
| The | The word the is the only definite article in the English language, and the most frequently used word in English the article the is often used as the very first part of a noun phrase in English. |

Chapter 3. Migration

Voluntary migration	Human migration is movement (physical or psychological) by humans from one district to another, sometimes over long distances or in large groups. The movement of populations in modern times has continued under the form of both voluntary migration within one's region, country, or beyond, and involuntary migration. People who migrate are called migrants, or, more specifically, emigrants, immigrants, or settlers, depending on historical setting, circumstances and perspective.
Crude birth rate	Crude birth rate is the nativity or childbirths per 1,000 people per year. According to the United Nations' World Population Prospects: The 2008 Revision Population Database, Crude birth rate(births in a period / population of person-years over that period). According to the Dictionary of Geography by Audrey Clark, Crude birth rate is also known as natural increase.
Demographic	Demographics data are the characteristics of a population as used in government, marketing or opinion research). Commonly-used Demographics include sex, race, age, income, disabilities, mobility (in terms of travel time to work or number of vehicles available), educational attainment, home ownership, employment status, and even location.
Ethnic	An ethnic group is a group of humans whose members identify with each other, through a common heritage that is real or assumed. This shared heritage may be based upon putative common ancestry, history, kinship, religion, language, shared territory, nationality or physical appearance. Members of an ethnic group are conscious of belonging to an ethnic group; moreover ethnic identity is further marked by the recognition from others of a group's distinctiveness.
Middle East	The Middle East is a region that encompasses southwestern Asia and Egypt. In some contexts, the term has recently been expanded in usage to sometimes include Pakistan and Afghanistan, the Caucacus, and North Africa. It's often used as a synonym for Near East, in opposition to Far East. The corresponding adjective is Middle-Eastern and the derived noun is Middle-Easterner.
Folk	The English word folk is derived from a Germanic noun *fulka meaning 'people' or 'army' (i.e. a crowd as opposed to 'a people' in a more abstract sense of clan or tribe). The English word folk has cognates in most of the other Germanic languages. folk may be a Germanic root that is unique to the Germanic languages, although Latin vulgus, 'the common people', has been suggested as a possible cognate.

Empire	The term Empire derives from the Latin imperium. Politically, an Empire is a geographically extensive group of states and peoples united and ruled either by a monarch (emperor, empress) or an oligarchy. Geopolitically, the term Empire has denoted very different, territorially-extreme states -- at the strong end, the extensive Spanish Empire and the British Empire (19th c.), at the weak end, the Holy Roman Empire (8th c.-19th c)., in its Medieval and early-modern forms, and the Byzantine Empire (15th c.), that was a direct continuation of the Roman Empire, that, in its final century of existence, was more a city-state than a territorial Empire.
Christianity	Christianity is a monotheistic religion based on the life and teachings of Jesus of Nazareth as presented in the New Testament. Christians believe Jesus is the son of God, God having become man and the savior of humanity. Christians, therefore, commonly refer to Jesus as Christ or Messiah.
Demographic transition	The Demographic transition model (DTM) is a model used to represent the process of explaining the transformation of countries from high birth rates and high death rates to low birth rates and low death rates as part of the economic development of a country from a pre-industrial to an industrialized economy. It is based on an interpretation begun in 1929 by the American demographer Warren Thompson of prior observed changes, or transitions, in birth and death rates in industrialized societies over the past two hundred years. Most developed countries are beyond stage three of the model; the majority of developing countries are in stage 2 or stage 3. The model was based on the changes seen in Europe so these countries follow the DTM relatively well.
Chain migration	Chain migration has two meanings. It refers to the social process by which immigrants from a particular town follow others from that town to a particular city or neighborhood, whether in an immigrant receiving country or in a new, usually urban, location in the home country. The term also refers to the process of foreign nationals immigrating to a new country under laws permitting their reunification with family members already living in the destination country.
Genocide	Genocide is the deliberate and systematic destruction, in whole or in part, of an ethnic, racial, religious, a legal definition is found in the 1948 United Nations Convention on the Prevention and Punishment of the Crime of Genocide (CPPCG` The preamble to the CPPCG states that instances of Genocide have taken place throughout history, but it was not until Raphael Lemkin coined the term and the prosecution of perpetrators of the Holocaust at the Nuremberg trials that the United Nations agreed to the CPPCG which defined the crime of Genocide under international law.

National Origins Act	The Immigration Act of 1924, or Johnson-Reed Act, including the National Origins Act, Asian Exclusion Act, (43 Statutes-at-Large 153) was a United States federal law that limited the number of immigrants who could be admitted from any country to 2% of the number of people from that country who were already living in the United States in 1890, according to the Census of 1890. It excluded immigration of Asians. It superseded the 1921 Emergency Quota Act. The law was aimed at further restricting the Southern and Eastern Europeans who were immigrating in large numbers starting in the 1890s, as well as prohibiting the immigration of East Asians and Asian Indians.
Immigration policy	An Immigration policy is any policy of a state that deals with the transit of persons across its borders, but especially those that intend to work and to remain in the country. Immigration policies can range from allowing no migration at all to allowing most types of migration, such as free immigration. Often, racial or religious bias is tied to Immigration policy (for example, a country might only allow commonwealth citizens admission).
Brain drain	Brain drain or human capital flight is a large emigration of individuals with technical skills or knowledge, normally due to conflict, lack of opportunity, political instability, since emigrants usually take with them the fraction of value of their training sponsored by the government. It is a parallel of capital flight which refers to the same movement of financial capital.
Guyana	Guyana officially the Co-operative Republic of Guyana and previously known as British Guiana, is a state on the northern coast of South America that is culturally part of the Anglophone Caribbean. Discovered by Europeans in 1498, Guyana`s past is punctuated by battles fought and won, possessions lost and regained as the Spanish, French, Dutch and British wrangled for centuries to own the land. It is the only state of the Commonwealth of Nations on mainland South America. Guyana is bordered to the east by Suriname, to the south and southwest by Brazil, to the west by Venezuela, and on the north by the Atlantic Ocean.
Luxembourg	Luxembourg , officially the Grand Duchy of Luxembourg , is a small, landlocked country in western Europe, bordered by Belgium, France, and Germany. Luxembourg has a population of under half a million people in an area of approximately 2,586 square kilometres . Luxembourg is a parliamentary representative democracy with a constitutional monarch; it is ruled by a Grand Duke.
Boat people	Boat people is a term that usually refers to illegal immigrants or asylum seekers who emigrate en masse in boats that are , rendering them unseaworthy and unsafe. The term came into common use during the late 1970s with the mass departure of Vietnamese refugees from Communist-controlled Vietnam, following the Vietnam War. Boat people from Haiti Boats have been a widely used form of migration or escape for people of limited resources.

Country	In geography, a Country is a geographical region. The term is often applied to a political division or the territory of a state, or to a smaller, or former, political division of a geographical region. Usually, but not always, a Country coincides with a sovereign territory and is associated with a state, nation and government.
Population	IV class="thumb tright"> Distribution of world Population in 1994. Time taken for each billion people to be added to the world`s Population (including future estimates).
Indonesia	The Republic of Indonesia is a country in Southeast Asia and Oceania. Indonesia comprises 17,508 islands. With a population of around 230 million people, it is the world`s fourth most populous country, with the world`s largest population of Muslims.
Rural	The term Rurals is used as an expression of different Rural areas as not being homogeneously defined. Many authors involved in mental health research in Rural areas, stress the importance of steering clear of inflexible blanket definitions of Rurality (Philo, 2003), and to instead `select definitions of Rurality that are appropriate to the study being conducted` (Cloke, 1977).
	Cloke`s index categorises all areas of England and Wales into four criteria: extreme Rural, intermediate Rural, intermediate non-Rural and extreme non-Rural; as well as urban areas.
Urban	Urban: An Urban area is an area with an increased density of human-created structures in comparison to the areas surrounding it. Urban areas are extremely dense population areas. An Urban area is more frequently called a city or metropolitan area.
Urban area	An Urban area is characterized by higher population density and vast human features in comparison to areas surrounding it. Urban areas may be cities, towns or conurbations, but the term is not commonly extended to rural settlements such as villages and hamlets.
	Urban areas are created and further developed by the process of urbanization.
Metropolitan area	A Metropolitan area is a large population center consisting of a large metropolis and its adjacent zone of influence, and the Metropolitan area is normally named after either the largest or most important central city within it.
	There has been no significant change in the basic Metropolitan area `concept` since its adoption in 1950 , though significant changes in geographic distributions have occurred since, and is expected to further evolve through time.

Popular culture	Popular culture is the totality of ideas, perspectives, attitudes, memes, images and other phenomena that are deemed preferred per an informal consensus within the mainstream of a given culture, specifically Western culture of the early to mid 20th century and the emerging global mainstream of the late 20th to 21st century. Heavily influenced by mass media, this collection of ideas permeates the everyday lives of the society. By contrast, folklore refers to the cultural mainstream of more local or pre-industrial societies.
Folk	The English word folk is derived from a Germanic noun *fulka meaning `people` or `army` (i.e. a crowd as opposed to `a people` in a more abstract sense of clan or tribe). The English word folk has cognates in most of the other Germanic languages. folk may be a Germanic root that is unique to the Germanic languages, although Latin vulgus, `the common people`, has been suggested as a possible cognate.
Diffusion	`Diffusion` is a time-dependent process , constituted by random motion of given entities and causing the statistical distribution of these entities to spread in space. The concept of Diffusion is tied to notion of mass transport, driven by a concentration gradient. The concept of Diffusion emerged in the physical sciences.
Demographic	Demographics data are the characteristics of a population as used in government, marketing or opinion research). Commonly-used Demographics include sex, race, age, income, disabilities, mobility (in terms of travel time to work or number of vehicles available), educational attainment, home ownership, employment status, and even location.
Demographic transition	The Demographic transition model (DTM) is a model used to represent the process of explaining the transformation of countries from high birth rates and high death rates to low birth rates and low death rates as part of the economic development of a country from a pre-industrial to an industrialized economy. It is based on an interpretation begun in 1929 by the American demographer Warren Thompson of prior observed changes, or transitions, in birth and death rates in industrialized societies over the past two hundred years. Most developed countries are beyond stage three of the model; the majority of developing countries are in stage 2 or stage 3. The model was based on the changes seen in Europe so these countries follow the DTM relatively well.
Nation	Nationalism appeared in Africa and Asia after World War I, led by politicians like Mustafa Kemal Atatürk. But only after World War II did its influence really become apparent in political processes, especially in the formation of states as a result of decolonization. In 1945, when the United Nations were founded, eight of its members were Asian states, and four, African.

Area studies	Area studies are interdisciplinary fields of research and scholarship pertaining to particular geographical, national/federal, in the practice of scholarship, many heterogeneous fields of research, encompassing both the social sciences and the humanities. Typical Area studies programs involve history, political science, sociology, cultural studies, languages, geography, literature, and related disciplines.
Cultural diversity	Cultural diversity is the variety of human societies or cultures in a specific region) There is a general consensus among mainstream anthropologists that humans first emerged in Africa about two million years ago .
Cultural ecology	Cultural ecology studies the relationship between a given society and its natural environment, the life-forms and ecosystems that support its lifeways. This may be carried out diachronically (examining entities that existed in different epochs), or synchronically (examining a present system and its components). The central argument is that the natural environment, in small scale or subsistence societies dependent in part upon it - is a major contributor to social organization and other human institutions.
Transylvania	Transylvania has had different names applied to it in several traditions. The first document in which the Medieval Latin term Ultra siluam is used in reference to the area dates from 1075. The term Partes Transsylvanæ (`parts beyond the forest`) dates from the same century . The names of Ardeal in Romanian and Erdély in Hungarian are believed to be connected.
Country	In geography, a Country is a geographical region. The term is often applied to a political division or the territory of a state, or to a smaller, or former, political division of a geographical region. Usually, but not always, a Country coincides with a sovereign territory and is associated with a state, nation and government.
Developed country	The term Developed country is used to describe countries that have a high level of development according to some criteria. Which criteria, and which countries are classified as being developed, is a contentious issue and there is fierce debate about this. Economic criteria have tended to dominate discussions.
Islam	Islam is the religion articulated by the Qur`an, a religious book considered by its adherents to be the verbatim word of the single incomparable God , and by the Prophet of Islam Muhammad`s demonstrations and real-life examples (called the Sunnah, collected through narration of his companions in collections of Hadith). Islam literally means submission to God . An adherent of Islam is a Muslim, meaning `one who submits (to God)`.

Ranch	A Ranch is an area of landscape, including various structures, given primarily to the practice of Ranching, the practice of raising grazing livestock such as cattle or sheep for meat or wool. The word most often applies to livestock-raising operations in the western United States and Canada, though there are Ranches in other areas. People who own or operate a Ranch are called stockgrowers or Ranchers.
Africa	Africa is the world's second-largest and second most-populous continent, after Asia. At about 30.2 million km^2 (11.7 million sq mi) including adjacent islands, it covers 6% of the Earth's total surface area and 20.4% of the total land area. With a billion people in 61 territories, it accounts for about 14.72% of the World's human population.
Middle East	The Middle East is a region that encompasses southwestern Asia and Egypt. In some contexts, the term has recently been expanded in usage to sometimes include Pakistan and Afghanistan, the Caucacus, and North Africa. It's often used as a synonym for Near East, in opposition to Far East. The corresponding adjective is Middle-Eastern and the derived noun is Middle-Easterner.
Taliban	The Taliban is a Sunni Islamist political movement that governed Afghanistan from 1996 until they were overthrown in late 2001 during Operation Enduring Freedom. It has regrouped since 2004 and revived as a strong insurgency movement governing at the local level and fighting a guerrilla war against the governments of Afghanistan, Pakistan, and the NATO-led International Security Assistance Force (ISAF). The movement is made up of members belonging to different ethnic Pashtun tribes, along with a number of volunteers from nearby Islamic countries such as Uzbeks, Tajiks, Chechens, Arabs, Punjabis and others.
Imperialism	Imperialism, defined by the dictionary of human geography, is 'the creation and maintenance of an unequal economic, cultural and territorial relationship, usually between states and often in the form of an empire, based on domination and subordination.' Imperialism, in many ways, is described as a primarily western concept that employs 'expansionist - capitalist - and latterly communist - systems.'
	Imperialism is considered the control by one state of other territories. Through political or military means (direct Imperialism), the imperial power may take over the government of a particular territory, or through economic processes (indirect Imperialism), in which the concerned region is officially self-governing but linked to the imperial power by, often unequal, trade relations. Furthermore, the notion of cultural Imperialism is indicated by 'existing or traditional ways of life and ways of thinking [that] are subordinated to the culture of the imperialists.'
	The term Imperialism commonly refers to a political or geographical domain such as the Ottoman Empire, the French Empire the Russian Empire, the Chinese Empire, or the British Empire, etc., but the term can equally be applied to domains of knowledge, beliefs, values and expertise, such as the empires of Christianity or Islam .

Bermuda Triangle	The Bermuda Triangle, also known as the Devil`s Triangle, is a region in the western part of the North Atlantic Ocean in which a number of aircraft and surface vessels are alleged to have mysteriously disappeared in a manner that cannot be explained by human error, piracy, equipment failure, a suspension of the laws of physics, or activity by extraterrestrial beings.
	A substantial body of documentation reveals, however, that a significant portion of the allegedly mysterious incidents have been inaccurately reported or embellished by later authors, and numerous official agencies have stated that the number and nature of disappearances in the region is similar to any other area of ocean.
Communism	Communism is a social structure in which classes are abolished and property is commonly controlled, as well as a political philosophy and social movement that advocates and aims to create such a society. Karl Marx, the father of communist thought, posited that communism would be the final stage in society, which would be achieved through a proletarian revolution and only possible after a socialist stage develops the productive forces, leading to a superabundance of goods and services.
	`Pure communism` in the Marxian sense refers to a classless, stateless and oppression-free society where decisions on what to produce and what policies to pursue are made democratically, allowing every member of society to participate in the decision-making process in both the political and economic spheres of life.

Ireland	Ireland ; Ulster Scots: Airlann, Latin: Hibernia) is the third-largest island in Europe and the twentieth-largest island in the world. It lies to the north-west of continental Europe and is surrounded by hundreds of islands and islets. To the east of Ireland, separated by the Irish Sea, is the island of Great Britain.
North Germanic	The North Germanic languages or Scandinavian languages make up one of the three branches of the Germanic languages, a sub-family of the Indo-European languages, along with the West Germanic languages and the extinct East Germanic languages. The language group is sometimes referred to as the Nordic languages, a direct translation of the most common term used among Danish, Swedish and Norwegian scholars and laypeople. In Scandinavia, Scandinavian language is also used as a term referring specifically to the mutually intelligible languages of the three Scandinavian countries.
Demographic	Demographics data are the characteristics of a population as used in government, marketing or opinion research). Commonly-used Demographics include sex, race, age, income, disabilities, mobility (in terms of travel time to work or number of vehicles available), educational attainment, home ownership, employment status, and even location.
Demographic transition	The Demographic transition model (DTM) is a model used to represent the process of explaining the transformation of countries from high birth rates and high death rates to low birth rates and low death rates as part of the economic development of a country from a pre-industrial to an industrialized economy. It is based on an interpretation begun in 1929 by the American demographer Warren Thompson of prior observed changes, or transitions, in birth and death rates in industrialized societies over the past two hundred years. Most developed countries are beyond stage three of the model; the majority of developing countries are in stage 2 or stage 3. The model was based on the changes seen in Europe so these countries follow the DTM relatively well.
Diffusion	`Diffusion` is a time-dependent process , constituted by random motion of given entities and causing the statistical distribution of these entities to spread in space. The concept of Diffusion is tied to notion of mass transport, driven by a concentration gradient. The concept of Diffusion emerged in the physical sciences.
Dialect	The term dialect is used in two distinct ways, even by scholars of language. One usage refers to a variety of a language that is characteristic of a particular group of the language`s speakers. The term is applied most often to regional speech patterns, but a dialect may also be defined by other factors, such as social class.

Scandinavian language	The North Germanic languages s make up one of the three branches of the Germanic languages, a sub-family of the Indo-European languages, along with the West Germanic languages and the extinct East Germanic languages. The language group is sometimes referred to as the Nordic languages, a direct translation of the most common term used among Danish, Swedish and Norwegian scholars and laypeople. In Scandinavia, Scandinavian language is also used as a term referring specifically to the mutually intelligible languages of the three Scandinavian countries.
West Germanic	The West Germanic languages constitute the largest of the three traditional branches of the Germanic family of languages and include languages such as English, Dutch and Afrikaans, German, the Frisian languages, and Yiddish. The other two of these three traditional branches of the Germanic languages are the North and East Germanic languages. The Germanic languages are traditionally divided into three groups: West, East and North Germanic.
Austro-Asiatic	The Austro-Asiatic languages are a large language family of Southeast Asia, and also scattered throughout India and Bangladesh. The name comes from the Latin word for `south` and the Greek name of Asia, hence `South Asia.` Among these languages, only Khmer, Vietnamese, and Mon have a long established recorded history, and only Vietnamese and Khmer have official status . The rest of the languages are spoken by minority groups.
Indo-Iranian languages	The Indo-Iranian language group constitutes the easternmost extant branch of the Indo-European family of languages. It consists of three language groups: the Indo-Aryan, Iranian and Nuristani. The term Aryan languages is occasionally still used to refer to the Indo-Iranian languages.
Communism	Communism is a social structure in which classes are abolished and property is commonly controlled, as well as a political philosophy and social movement that advocates and aims to create such a society. Karl Marx, the father of communist thought, posited that communism would be the final stage in society, which would be achieved through a proletarian revolution and only possible after a socialist stage develops the productive forces, leading to a superabundance of goods and services. `Pure communism` in the Marxian sense refers to a classless, stateless and oppression-free society where decisions on what to produce and what policies to pursue are made democratically, allowing every member of society to participate in the decision-making process in both the political and economic spheres of life.
Balto-Slavic	The Balto-Slavic language group consists of the Baltic and Slavic languages, belonging to the Indo-European family of languages. Having experienced a period of common development, Baltic and Slavic languages share several linguistic traits not found in any other Indo-European branch, which points to their close genetic relationship.

A hypothetical Proto-Balto-Slavic language is also reconstructable, descending from Proto-Indo-European by means of well-defined sound laws, and out of which modern Slavic and Baltic languages descended.

Croatia

Croatia , officially the Republic of Croatia is a country in central and southeastern Europe, at the crossroads of the Pannonian Plain, the Balkans, and the Mediterranean Sea. Its capital (and largest city) is Zagreb. Croatia borders Slovenia and Hungary to the north, Bosnia and Herzegovina to the southeast, and Serbia and Montenegro to the east.

Herzegovina

Herzegovina is the southern region of Bosnia-Herzegovina, comprising 11,419 sq km or around 22% of the total area of the present-day country. In other sources it comprises 12,276 sq km, this constitutes 24% of Bosnia and Herzegovina. There is no official border distinguishing it from the Bosnian region, though it is generally accepted that the borders of the region are Croatia to the west, Montenegro to the south, the canton boundaries of the Herzegovina-Neretva Canton in the east and Gornji Vakuf-Uskoplje in the north.

Iran

The Islamic Republic of Iran has a comprehensive and effective program of family planning. While Iran's population grew at a rate of more than 3%/year between 1956 and 1986, the growth rate began to decline in the late 1980s and early 1990s after the government initiated a major population control program. By 2007 the growth rate had declined to 0.7 percent per year, with a birth rate of 17 per 1,000 persons and a death rate of 6 per 1,000. Reports by the UN show birth control policies in Iran to be effective with the country topping the list of greatest fertility decreases.

Empire

The term Empire derives from the Latin imperium. Politically, an Empire is a geographically extensive group of states and peoples united and ruled either by a monarch (emperor, empress) or an oligarchy. Geopolitically, the term Empire has denoted very different, territorially-extreme states -- at the strong end, the extensive Spanish Empire and the British Empire (19th c.)., at the weak end, the Holy Roman Empire (8th c.-19th c.), in its Medieval and early-modern forms, and the Byzantine Empire (15th c.)., that was a direct continuation of the Roman Empire, that, in its final century of existence, was more a city-state than a territorial Empire.

Hebrew

Hebrew is a Semitic language of the Afro-Asiatic language family. Culturally, it is considered a Jewish language. Hebrew in its modern form is spoken by more than seven million people in Israel while Classical Hebrew has been used for prayer or study in Jewish communities around the world for over two thousand years.

Austronesian

The Austronesian languages are a language family widely dispersed throughout the islands of Southeast Asia and the Pacific, with a few members spoken on continental Asia. It is on par with Bantu, Indo-European, Afro-Asiatic and Uralic as one of the best-established ancient language families. The name Austronesian comes from Latin auster `south wind` plus Greek nêsos `island`.

Niger-Congo	The Niger-Congo languages constitute one of the world`s major language families, and Africa`s largest in terms of geographical area, number of speakers, and number of distinct languages. They may constitute the world`s largest language family in terms of distinct languages, although this question is complicated by ambiguity about what constitutes a distinct language. Most of the most widely spoken indigenous languages of Subsaharan Africa belong to this group.
Immigration	Immigration is the arrival of new individuals into a habitat or population. It is a biological concept and is important in population ecology, differentiated from emigration and migration.
	The International Organization for Migration or(I.O.M) said there are more than 200 million migrants around the world today.
Afro-Asiatic	The Afroasiatic languages constitute a language family with about 375 living languages (SIL estimate) and more than 350 million speakers spread throughout North Africa, the Horn of Africa, and Southwest Asia, as well as parts of the Sahel, West Africa and East Africa. The most widely spoken Afroasiatic language is Arabic, with over 280 million native speakers . In addition to languages now spoken, Afroasiatic includes several ancient languages, such as Ancient Egyptian, Biblical Hebrew, and Akkadian.
	The term `Afroasiatic` (often now spelled as Afro-Asiatic) was coined by Maurice Delafosse (1914).
Buddhism	Buddhism is a religion and philosophy encompassing a variety of traditions, beliefs and practices, largely based on teachings attributed to Siddhartha Gautama, commonly known as the Buddha . Buddha lived and taught in the northeastern Indian subcontinent sometime between the 6th and 4th centuries BCE. He is recognized by adherents as an awakened teacher who shared his insights to help sentient beings end suffering, achieve nirvana, and escape what is seen as a cycle of suffering and rebirth.
	Two major branches of Buddhism are recognized: Theravada and Mahayana (`The Great Vehicle`).
Korea	Korea (Korean: í•œêµ or ì¡°ì„) is a civilization and formerly unified nation currently divided into two states. Located on the Korean Peninsula, it borders China to the northwest, Russia to the northeast, and is separated from Japan to the east by the Korea Strait.
	Korea was united until 1948; at that time it was split into South Korea and North Korea.
Bashkir language	The Bashkir language is a Turkic language, and is the language of the Bashkirs.

Speakers of the Bashkir language mostly live in the Russian republic of Bashkortostan. Substantial number of the speakers also live in Chelyabinsk, Orenburg, Sverdlovsk, Samara and Kurgan Oblasts, Khanty-Mansi Autonomous Okrug--Yugra, Tatarstan and Udmurtia.

Uralic	The Uralic languages constitute a language family of 39 languages spoken by approximately 25 million people. The healthiest Uralic languages in terms of the number of native speakers are Hungarian, Finnish, Estonian, Mari and Udmurt. Countries that are home to a significant number of speakers of Uralic languages include Estonia, Finland, Hungary, Romania, Russia, Serbia and Slovakia.
The	The word the is the only definite article in the English language, and the most frequently used word in English the article the is often used as the very first part of a noun phrase in English.
Mongolian language	The Mongolian language is the best-known member of the Mongolic language family. It has about 5.7 million speakers, including over 90% of the residents of Mongolia and many of the Mongolian residents of the Inner Mongolia autonomous region of China. In Mongolia, the Khalkha dialect of Mongolian, written in Cyrillic, is predominant; in Inner Mongolia, the language is more dialectally diverse and written in the traditional Mongolian script.
Fur	The Fur are an ethnic group from western Sudan, principally inhabiting the region of DarFur, where they are the largest tribe. They are a Western Sudanese people who practice sedentary herding and agriculture, mainly the cultivation of millet. Their society is a traditional one governed by village elders.
Khoisan	Khoisan is a unifying name for two major ethnic groups of Southern Africa. Historically, they have been referred to as the Capoid race because they can be visually distinguished from most other sub-Saharan Africans by way of their relatively lighter skin color and their epicanthic folds. From the beginning of the Upper Paleolithic period, hunting and gathering cultures known as the Sangoan occupied southern Africa in areas where annual rainfall is less than 40 inches (1016mm)--and today`s San and Khoi people resemble the ancient Sangoan skeletal remains. The Khoisan people were the original inhabitants of much of southern Africa before the southward Bantu expansion -- coming down the east and west coasts of Africa -- and later European colonization.
Khoisan languages	The Khoisan languages are the click languages of Africa, which do not belong to other language families. They include languages indigenous to southern and eastern Africa, though some, such as the Khoi languages, appear to have moved to their current locations not long before the Bantu expansion. In southern Africa their speakers are the Khoi and Bushmen (Saan), in east Africa the Sandawe and Hadza.

Niger-Congo languages	The Niger-Congo languages constitute one of the world's major language families, and Africa's largest in terms of geographical area, number of speakers, and number of distinct languages. They may constitute the world's largest language family in terms of distinct languages, although this question is complicated by ambiguity about what constitutes a distinct language. Most of the most widely spoken indigenous languages of Subsaharan Africa belong to this group.
Nilo-Saharan	The Nilo-Saharan languages are African languages spoken mainly in the upper parts of the Chari and Nile rivers (hence the term `Nilo-`), including historic Nubia, north of where the two tributaries of Nile meet. The languages extend through 17 nations in the northern half of Africa: from Algeria and Mali in the northwest; to Benin, Nigeria and the Democratic Republic of the Congo in the south; and Sudan to Tanzania in the east (excluding the Horn of Africa).
	The largest part of its major subfamilies are found in the modern nation of Sudan, through which the Nile River flows in all its incarnations: the White and Blue Nile, which join to form the main Nile at Khartoum.
Nilo-Saharan languages	The Nilo-Saharan languages are African languages spoken mainly in the upper parts of the Chari and Nile rivers (hence the term `Nilo-`), including historic Nubia, north of where the two tributaries of Nile meet. The languages extend through 17 nations in the northern half of Africa: from Algeria and Mali in the northwest; to Benin, Nigeria and the Democratic Republic of the Congo in the south; and Sudan to Tanzania in the east (excluding the Horn of Africa).
	The largest part of its major subfamilies are found in the modern nation of Sudan, through which the Nile River flows in all its incarnations: the White and Blue Nile, which join to form the main Nile at Khartoum.
Swahili	Swahili is a Bantu language spoken by various ethnic groups that inhabit several large stretches of the Indian Ocean coastline from southern Somalia to northern Mozambique, including the Comoros Islands. Although only 5-10 million people speak it as their native language, Swahili is also a lingua franca of much of East Africa and the Democratic Republic of the Congo, is a national or official language of four nations, and is the only language of African origin among the official working languages of the African Union.
	Swahili is a Bantu language that serves as a second language to various groups traditionally inhabiting parts of the East African coast.
Ethnic	An ethnic group is a group of humans whose members identify with each other, through a common heritage that is real or assumed. This shared heritage may be based upon putative common ancestry, history, kinship, religion, language, shared territory, nationality or physical appearance. Members of an ethnic group are conscious of belonging to an ethnic group; moreover ethnic identity is further marked by the recognition from others of a group's distinctiveness.

Nigeria	Nigeria, officially the Federal Republic of Nigeria, is a federal constitutional republic comprising thirty-six states and one Federal Capital Territory. The country is located in West Africa and shares land borders with the Republic of Benin in the west, Chad and Cameroon in the east, and Niger in the north. Its coast lies on the Gulf of Guinea, a part of the Atlantic Ocean, in the south.
Middle East	The Middle East is a region that encompasses southwestern Asia and Egypt. In some contexts, the term has recently been expanded in usage to sometimes include Pakistan and Afghanistan, the Caucacus, and North Africa. It's often used as a synonym for Near East, in opposition to Far East. The corresponding adjective is Middle-Eastern and the derived noun is Middle-Easterner.
Flanders	Flanders (Dutch: Â·), French: Flandre) is the community of the Flemings but also one of the institutions in Belgium, and a geographical region located in parts of present-day Belgium, France, and the Netherlands. Over the course of history, the geographical territory that was called `Flanders` has varied. In contemporary Belgium, Flanders might be understood as the `country of the Flemings`.
Pidgin	A pidgin language is a simplified language that develops as a means of communication between two or more groups that do not have a language in common, in situations such as trade, or where both groups speak languages different than the language of the country in which they reside (but there is no common language between the groups). A `pidgin` language is, fundamentally, a simplified means of linguistic communication, as is constructed impromptu, or by convention, between groups of people. A `pidgin` language is not the native language of any speech community, but is instead learned as a second language.

Country	In geography, a Country is a geographical region. The term is often applied to a political division or the territory of a state, or to a smaller, or former, political division of a geographical region. Usually, but not always, a Country coincides with a sovereign territory and is associated with a state, nation and government.
Developed country	The term Developed country is used to describe countries that have a high level of development according to some criteria. Which criteria, and which countries are classified as being developed, is a contentious issue and there is fierce debate about this. Economic criteria have tended to dominate discussions.
Christianity	Christianity is a monotheistic religion based on the life and teachings of Jesus of Nazareth as presented in the New Testament.
	Christians believe Jesus is the son of God, God having become man and the savior of humanity. Christians, therefore, commonly refer to Jesus as Christ or Messiah.
Eastern Orthodox Church	The Orthodox Church, also officially called the Orthodox Catholic Church and commonly referred to in English-speaking countries as the Eastern Orthodox Church, is the world`s second largest Christian communion, estimated to number 300 million members .
	It sees itself as the One, Holy, Catholic and Apostolic Church established by Jesus Christ and his Apostles almost 2,000 years ago. The Church is composed of several self-governing ecclesial bodies, each geographically and nationally distinct but theologically unified.
Ethnic	An ethnic group is a group of humans whose members identify with each other, through a common heritage that is real or assumed. This shared heritage may be based upon putative common ancestry, history, kinship, religion, language, shared territory, nationality or physical appearance. Members of an ethnic group are conscious of belonging to an ethnic group; moreover ethnic identity is further marked by the recognition from others of a group`s distinctiveness.
Russian Orthodox Church	The Russian Orthodox Church; or The Moscow Patriarchate , or ÐœÐ¾ÑÐºÐ¾Ð²ÑÐºÐ¸Ð¹ ÐŸÐ°Ñ‚Ñ€Ð¸Ð°Ñ…Ð°Ñ‚ (Moskovskiy Patriarkhat) (the latter designation being another official name) since 1943, ÐŸÐ¾Ð¼ÐµÑÑ‚Ð½Ð°Ñ Ð Ð¾ÑÑÐ¸Ð¹ÑÐºÐ°Ñ ÐŸÑ€Ð° Ð²Ð¾ÑÐ»Ð°Ð²Ð½Ð°Ñ Ð¦ÐµÑ€ÐºÐ¾Ð²ÑŒ (Pomestnaya Rossiyskaya Pravoslavnaya Tserkov) before the reinstitution in 1943), also known as the Orthodox Christian Church of Russia, is a body of Christians who constitute an autocephalous Eastern Orthodox Church under the jurisdiction of the Patriarch of Moscow, in communion with the other Eastern Orthodox Churches.

The Russian Orthodox Church is often said to be the largest of the Eastern Orthodox churches in the world and second only to the Roman Catholic Church among Christian churches, numbering over 135 million members world wide and growing numerically since late 1980s. Up to 65% of ethnic Russians and a significant number of Belarusians and Ukrainians identify themselves as `Orthodox`.

Islam	Islam is the religion articulated by the Qur`an, a religious book considered by its adherents to be the verbatim word of the single incomparable God , and by the Prophet of Islam Muhammad`s demonstrations and real-life examples (called the Sunnah, collected through narration of his companions in collections of Hadith). Islam literally means submission to God .
	An adherent of Islam is a Muslim, meaning `one who submits (to God)`.
Ramadan	Ramadan is the ninth month of the Islamic calendar. It is the Islamic month of fasting, in which participating Muslims refrain from eating, drinking, smoking, and indulging in anything that is in excess or ill-natured; from dawn until sunset. Fasting is meant to teach the Muslim patience, modesty and spirituality.
Taliban	The Taliban is a Sunni Islamist political movement that governed Afghanistan from 1996 until they were overthrown in late 2001 during Operation Enduring Freedom. It has regrouped since 2004 and revived as a strong insurgency movement governing at the local level and fighting a guerrilla war against the governments of Afghanistan, Pakistan, and the NATO-led International Security Assistance Force (ISAF). The movement is made up of members belonging to different ethnic Pashtun tribes, along with a number of volunteers from nearby Islamic countries such as Uzbeks, Tajiks, Chechens, Arabs, Punjabis and others.
Buddhism	Buddhism is a religion and philosophy encompassing a variety of traditions, beliefs and practices, largely based on teachings attributed to Siddhartha Gautama, commonly known as the Buddha . Buddha lived and taught in the northeastern Indian subcontinent sometime between the 6th and 4th centuries BCE. He is recognized by adherents as an awakened teacher who shared his insights to help sentient beings end suffering, achieve nirvana, and escape what is seen as a cycle of suffering and rebirth.
	Two major branches of Buddhism are recognized: Theravada and Mahayana (`The Great Vehicle`).
Four Noble Truths	The Four Noble Truths is one of the most fundamental Buddhist teachings. This Dharma Enlightenment makes ordinary person become the Buddha . In broad terms, these truths relate to suffering (or dukkha), its nature, its origin, its cessation and the path leading to its cessation.
Nation	Nationalism appeared in Africa and Asia after World War I, led by politicians like Mustafa Kemal Atatürk. But only after World War II did its influence really become apparent in political processes, especially in the formation of states as a result of decolonization.

In 1945, when the United Nations were founded, eight of its members were Asian states, and four, African.

Nation of Islam	The Nation of Islam is a religious organization founded in Detroit, Michigan by Wallace D. Fard Muhammad in July 1930, with the goal of resurrecting the spiritual, mental, social, and economic condition of the black men and women of America. The N.O.I. also promotes the belief that God will bring about a universal government of peace. Mainstream Muslims consider the group an independent religion that has adopted Islamic terminology rather than as an Islamic sect due to the differing beliefs of the concept of God, race, prophecy, and many others. However, in recent years the group has come a little closer to orthodox Islam by observing Ramadan and the Friday prayers.
Organization of Afro-American Unity	The Organization of Afro-American Unity was an organization formed by Malcolm X to promote cooperation between African-Americans. On June 28, 1964, six weeks after Malcolm X`s return to New York from Africa, he announced the formation of the Organization of Afro-American Unity. `It was formed in my living room,` remembers John Henrik Clarke.
Punjab	The Punjab , also spelled Panjab , is a cultural region straddling the border between Punjab and Punjab (India). The so-called `five waters` are the Jhelum, the Chenab, the Ravi, the Sutlej, and the Indus per se. All are tributaries of the Indus River, the Jhelum being the largest.
Judaism	Judaism is a set of beliefs and practices originating in the Hebrew Bible, also known as the Tanakh, and explored and explained in later texts such as the Talmud. Jews consider Judaism to be the expression of the covenantal relationship God developed with the Children of Israel-- originally a group of around a dozen tribes claiming descent from the Biblical patriarch Jacob and later the Jewish people. According to most branches, God revealed his laws and commandments to Moses on Mount Sinai in the form of both the Written and Oral Torah.
Africa	Africa is the world`s second-largest and second most-populous continent, after Asia. At about 30.2 million km$^2$ (11.7 million sq mi) including adjacent islands, it covers 6% of the Earth`s total surface area and 20.4% of the total land area. With a billion people in 61 territories, it accounts for about 14.72% of the World`s human population.
Animism	Animism is a philosophical, religious or spiritual idea that souls or spirits exist not only in humans but also in other animals, plants, rocks, natural phenomena such as thunder, geographic features such as mountains or rivers, or other entities of the natural environment. Animism may further attribute souls to abstract concepts such as words, true names or metaphors in mythology. Animism is particularly widely found in the religions of indigenous peoples, although it is also found in Shinto, and some forms of Hinduism and Neopaganism.

Abu Bakr	Abu Bakr As-Siddiq (Abdallah ibn Abi Quhafa) was Muhammad`s father-in-law, one of the closest companions and adviser. Abu Bakar succeeded to the Prophet`s political and administrative functions, thereby initiating the office of the caliphate. He was also the first convert to Islam, after Khadija, Muhammad`s first wife.
Khomeini	Syed Ruhollah Mousavi Khomeini was an Iranian religious leader and politician, and leader of the 1979 Iranian Revolution which saw the overthrow of Mohammad Reza Pahlavi, the Shah of Iran. Following the revolution and a national referendum, Khomeini became the country`s Supreme Leader--a position created in the constitution as the highest ranking political and religious authority of the nation--until his death.
	Khomeini was a marja or marja al-taqlid (`source of emulation`, also known as a Grand Ayatollah) in Twelver Shi`a Islam, but is most famous for his political role.
Lumbini	LumbinÄ« is a Buddhist pilgrimage site in the Rupandehi district of Nepal, near the Indian border. It is the place where Queen Mayadevi is said to have given birth to Siddhartha Gautama, who as the Buddha Gautama founded the Buddhist tradition. The Buddha lived between roughly 563 and 483 BCE. Lumbini is one of four magnets for pilgrimage that sprang up in places pivotal to the life of the Buddha, the others being at Kushinagar, Bodh Gaya, and Sarnath.
Diffusion	`Diffusion` is a time-dependent process , constituted by random motion of given entities and causing the statistical distribution of these entities to spread in space. The concept of Diffusion is tied to notion of mass transport, driven by a concentration gradient.
	The concept of Diffusion emerged in the physical sciences.
World Heritage Site	A UNESCO World Heritage Site is a site (such as a forest, mountain, lake, desert, monument, building, complex) that is on the list that is maintained by the international World Heritage Programme administered by the UNESCO World Heritage Committee, composed of 21 state parties which are elected by their General Assembly for a four-year term. A World Heritage Site is a place of either cultural or physical significance.
	The program catalogues, names, and conserves sites of outstanding cultural or natural importance to the common heritage of humanity.
Lake	A Lake is a terrain feature , a body of liquid on the surface of a world that is localized to the bottom of basin (another type of landform or terrain feature; that is, it is not global) and moves slowly if it moves at all. Another definition is, a body of fresh or salt water of considerable size that is surrounded by land. On Earth, a body of water is considered a Lake when it is inland, not part of the ocean, is larger and deeper than a pond, and is fed by a river.

Salt Lake	A Salt lake or saline lake is a landlocked body of water which has a concentration of salts and other minerals significantly higher than most lakes (often defined as at least three grams of salt per liter). In some cases, Salt lakes have a higher concentration of salt than sea water, but such lakes would also be termed hypersaline lakes. Salt lakes form when the water flowing into the lake, containing salt or minerals, cannot leave because the lake is endorheic (terminal).
Empire	The term Empire derives from the Latin imperium. Politically, an Empire is a geographically extensive group of states and peoples united and ruled either by a monarch (emperor, empress) or an oligarchy. Geopolitically, the term Empire has denoted very different, territorially-extreme states -- at the strong end, the extensive Spanish Empire and the British Empire (19th c.), at the weak end, the Holy Roman Empire (8th c.-19th c)., in its Medieval and early-modern forms, and the Byzantine Empire (15th c.), that was a direct continuation of the Roman Empire, that, in its final century of existence, was more a city-state than a territorial Empire.
Middle East	The Middle East is a region that encompasses southwestern Asia and Egypt. In some contexts, the term has recently been expanded in usage to sometimes include Pakistan and Afghanistan, the Caucacus, and North Africa. It`s often used as a synonym for Near East, in opposition to Far East. The corresponding adjective is Middle-Eastern and the derived noun is Middle-Easterner.
Diaspora	A Diaspora is any movement of a population sharing common ethnic identity. While refugees may or may not ultimately settle in a new geographic location, the term Diaspora refers to a permanently displaced and relocated collective. Diasporic cultural development often assumes a different course from that of the population in the original place of settlement.
Holy places	Holy places, generally refers to the sites that a religion considers to be of special religious significance. They are usually places visited by pilgrims. .
Jewish	Judaism is a set of beliefs and practices originating in the Hebrew Bible, also known as the Tanakh, and explored and explained in later texts such as the Talmud. Jews consider Judaism to be the expression of the covenantal relationship God developed with the Children of Israel-- originally a group of around a dozen tribes claiming descent from the Biblical patriarch Jacob and later the Jewish people. According to most branches, God revealed his laws and commandments to Moses on Mount Sinai in the form of both the Written and Oral Torah.
Ghetto	Originally used in Venice to describe the area where Jews were compelled to live, a Ghetto is now described as a `portion of a city in which members of a minority group live; especially because of social, legal, or economic pressure.`

The word `Ghetto` actually comes from the word `getto` or `gheto`, which means slag in Venetian, and was used in this sense in a reference to a foundry where slag was stored located on the same island as the area of Jewish confinement. An alternative etymology is from Italian borGhetto, diminutive of borgo `borough`.

The corresponding German term was Judengasse known as the Jewish Quarter.

Shrine

A Shrine is a holy or sacred place, which is dedicated to a specific deity, ancestor, hero, martyr, saint or similar figure of awe and respect, at which they are venerated or worshipped. Shrines often contain idols, relics, or other such objects associated with the figure being venerated. A Shrine at which votive offerings are made is called an altar.

Park

A Park is a protected area, in its natural or semi-natural state or planted, and set aside for human recreation and enjoyment. It may consist of, rocks, soil, water, flora and fauna and grass areas.

Wilderness Parks are intact and undeveloped areas used mainly by wild species.

ÅšrÄ□vastÄ«

ÅšrÄ□vastÄ« or SÄ□vatthÄ« , a city of ancient India, was one of the six largest cities in India during Gautama Buddha`s lifetime. The city was located in the fertile Gangetic plains in the present day`s Gonda district of Uttar Pradesh. Jetavana monastery was a famous monastery close to Savatthi.

Indira Priyadarshini Gandhi

Indira Priyadarshini Gandhi (Hindi: à¤‡à¤¨à¦¿à¤°à¤¾ à¤ªà¥□à¤°à¤¿à¤¯à¤¦à¤° à¥□à¤¶à¿à¨¨à¥€ à¤—à¤¾à¤,à¤§à¥€ IndirÄ□ PriyadarÅ›inÄ« GÄ□ndhÄ«; née: Nehru; (19 November 1917 - 31 October 1984) was the prime minister of the Republic of India for three consecutive terms from 1966 to 1977 and for a fourth term from 1980 until her assassination in 1984, a total of fifteen years. She was India`s first, and to date only, female prime minister.

Gandhi was partly educated in India and then in Britain: at Badminton School, a girls` independent school in Bristol, and at Somerville College at the University of Oxford.

Hajj

The Hajj is a pilgrimage in Mecca. It is currently the largest annual pilgrimage in the world, and is the fifth pillar of Islam, a religious duty that must be carried out at least once in their lifetime by every able-bodied Muslim who can afford to do so. The Hajj is a demonstration of the solidarity of the Muslim people, and their submission to God . The pilgrimage occurs from the 7th to 13th day of Dhu al-Hijjah, the 12th month of the Islamic calendar.

Israel	Israel officially the State of Israel , Medinat Yisra`el; Arabic: Ø¯ÙŽÙˆÙ„ÙŽØ©Ù Ø¥ÙØ³Ù’Ø±ÙŽØ§Ù¦ÙÙŠÙ„ÙŽâ€Ž, Dawlat IsrÄ`Ä«l), is a developed country in Western Asia located on the eastern shore of the Mediterranean Sea. It borders Lebanon in the north, Syria in the northeast, Jordan in the east, and Egypt on the southwest, and contains geographically diverse features within its relatively small area. Also adjacent are the West Bank to the east and Gaza Strip to the southwest.
Minaret	Minarets are distinctive architectural features of Islamic mosques- generally tall spires with onion-shaped or conical crowns, usually either free standing or taller than any associated support structure; the basic form includes a base, shaft, and gallery. Styles vary regionally and by period. They provide a visual focal point and are used for the call to prayer (adhan).
Catacombs	Catacombs are ancient, human-made underground passageways or subterranean cemeteries composed thereof. Many are under cities and have served during historic times as a refuge for safety during wars or as a meeting place for cults. The first burial galleries to be referred to as Catacombs lie beneath San Sebastiano fuori le mura, in Rome.
Cemetery	A Cemetery is a place in which dead bodies and cremated remains are buried. The term Cemetery implies that the land is specifically designated as a burying ground. Cemeteries in the Western world are the place where the final ceremonies of death are observed.
The	The word the is the only definite article in the English language, and the most frequently used word in English the article the is often used as the very first part of a noun phrase in English.
Archbishop	In Roman Catholicism, an archbishop is an elevated bishop. In many Roman Churches, this means that they lead a diocese of particular importance called an archdiocese. An archbishop is equivalent to a bishop in sacred matters but simply has a higher precedence or degree of prestige.
Diocese	In some forms of Christianity, a Diocese is an administrative territorial unit administered by a bishop. It is also referred to as a bishopric or Episcopal Area (as in United Methodism) or episcopal see, though strictly the term episcopal see refers to the domain of ecclesiastical authority officially held by the bishop, and bishopric to the post of being bishop. The Diocese is the key geographical unit of authority in the form of church governance known as episcopal polity.
Communism	Communism is a social structure in which classes are abolished and property is commonly controlled, as well as a political philosophy and social movement that advocates and aims to create such a society. Karl Marx, the father of communist thought, posited that communism would be the final stage in society, which would be achieved through a proletarian revolution and only possible after a socialist stage develops the productive forces, leading to a superabundance of goods and services.

`Pure communism` in the Marxian sense refers to a classless, stateless and oppression-free society where decisions on what to produce and what policies to pursue are made democratically, allowing every member of society to participate in the decision-making process in both the political and economic spheres of life.

Ireland

Ireland ; Ulster Scots: Airlann, Latin: Hibernia) is the third-largest island in Europe and the twentieth-largest island in the world. It lies to the north-west of continental Europe and is surrounded by hundreds of islands and islets. To the east of Ireland, separated by the Irish Sea, is the island of Great Britain.

Irish Republican Army

The Irish Republican Army was an Irish republican revolutionary military organisation. It was descended from the Irish Volunteers, an organisation established on 25 November 1913 that staged the Easter Rising in April 1916. In 1919, the Irish Republic that had been proclaimed during the Easter Rising was formally established by an elected assembly (Dáil Éireann),and the Irish Volunteers were recognised by Dáil Éireann as its legitimate army. Thereafter, the Irish Republican Army waged a guerrilla campaign against British rule in Ireland in the 1919-21 Irish War of Independence.

Marxism

Marxism is a particular political philosophy, economic and sociological worldview based upon a materialist interpretation of history, a Marxist analysis of capitalism, a theory of social change, and an atheist view of human liberation derived from the work of Karl Marx and Friedrich Engels. The three primary aspects of Marxism are:

· The dialectical and materialist concept of history -- Humankind`s history is fundamentally that of the struggle between social classes. The productive capacity of society is the foundation of society, and as this capacity increases over time the social relations of production, class relations, evolve through this struggle of the classes and pass through definite stages (primitive communism, slavery, feudalism, capitalism). The legal, political, ideological and other aspects (ex.

Ulster

Ulster (Irish: Ulaidh / Cúige Uladh, Ulster Scots: Ulstèr) is one of the four Provinces of Ireland, located in the north of the island.

Ulster is composed of nine counties: Antrim, Armagh, Down, Fermanagh, Londonderry, and Tyrone are part of Northern Ireland; while Cavan, Donegal, and Monaghan are part of the Republic of Ireland.

The first part of the name Ulster derives from the Irish Cúige Uladh (IPA: [ЁˆkuЁˆ□ÉŸ ЁˆÊˆŒIЁˆ u, ЁˆÊˆŒIЁˆ i]), meaning `Fifth of the Ulaid`.

Crusade	The Crusades were a series of religiously-sanctioned military campaigns waged by much of Latin Christian Europe, particularly the Franks of France and the Holy Roman Empire. The specific Crusades to restore Christian control of the Holy Land were fought over a period of nearly 200 years, between 1095 and 1291. Other campaigns in Spain and Eastern Europe continued into the 15th century. The Crusades were fought mainly against Muslims, although campaigns were also waged against pagan Slavs, Jews, Russian and Greek Orthodox Christians, Mongols, Cathars, Hussites, Waldensians, Old Prussians, and political enemies of the popes.

Jerusalem on the map of Israel.

Jerusalem	Israeli Metropolitan Area: 1,029,300 (*2009*)
Area	125,156 dunams (125.156 km^2; 48.323 sq mi)
Mayor	Nir Barkat
Coordinates	31°47′N 35°13′Eï»¿ / ï»¿31.783°N 35.217°ECoordinates: 31°47′N 35°13′Eï»¿ / ï»¿31.783°N 35.217°E
Website	www.Jerusalem.muni.il
	Jerusalem , Yerushaláyim; Arabic: ال‫ÙÙ,ÙØ¯ Ø³ Â·), al-Quds) is the capital of Israel and its largest city in both population and area, with a population of 763,800 residents over an area of 125.1 km^2 if disputed East Jerusalem is included. Located in the Judean Mountains, between the Mediterranean Sea and the northern edge of the Dead Sea, modern Jerusalem has grown far beyond the boundaries of the Old City. The city has a history that goes back to the 4th millennium BCE, making it one of the oldest cities in the world.

Dome	A Dome is a structural element of architecture that resembles the hollow upper half of a sphere. Dome structures made of various materials have a long architectural lineage extending into prehistory. Corbel Domes have been found in the ancient Middle East in modest buildings and tombs.
Holy Land	The Holy Land , generally refers to the geographical region of the Levant called Land of Canaan or Land of Israel in the Bible, and constitutes the Promised land. This area, or sites within it, hold significant religious importance to at least four monotheistic Abrahamic religions: Judaism, Christianity, Islam and the Bahá`í Faith. Part of its sanctity stems from the religious significance of Jerusalem, the holiest city to Judaism, the third-holiest to Islam, and part of the proposed Christian Pentarchy.
Palestine Liberation Organization	The Palestine Liberation Organization is a political and once was considered organization founded in 1964. It is recognized as the `sole legitimate representative of the Palestinian people,` by over 100 states with which it holds diplomatic relations, and has enjoyed observer status at the United Nations since 1974. In 1993 Israel also officially recognized the Palestine Liberation Organization as the representative of the Palestinian people.

Founded by a meeting of 422 Palestinian national figures in the West Bank, in May 1964, following an earlier decision of the Arab League, its goal was the liberation of Palestine through armed struggle. The original Palestine Liberation Organization Charter stated that `Palestine with its boundaries that existed at the time of the British mandate is an integral regional unit` and sought to `prohibit...

Chapter 7. Ethnicity

Africa	Africa is the world`s second-largest and second most-populous continent, after Asia. At about 30.2 million km$^2$ (11.7 million sq mi) including adjacent islands, it covers 6% of the Earth`s total surface area and 20.4% of the total land area. With a billion people in 61 territories, it accounts for about 14.72% of the World`s human population.
Ethnic	An ethnic group is a group of humans whose members identify with each other, through a common heritage that is real or assumed. This shared heritage may be based upon putative common ancestry, history, kinship, religion, language, shared territory, nationality or physical appearance. Members of an ethnic group are conscious of belonging to an ethnic group; moreover ethnic identity is further marked by the recognition from others of a group`s distinctiveness.
Alaska	Alaska is the largest state of the United States of America by area; it is situated in the northwest extremity of the North American continent, with Canada to the east, the Arctic Ocean to the north, and the Pacific Ocean to the west and south, with Russia further west across the Bering Strait. Approximately half of Alaska`s 683,478 residents reside within the Anchorage metropolitan area. As of 2009, Alaska remains the least densely populated state of the U.S. The U.S. Senate approved the purchase of Alaska from the Russian Empire on March 30, 1867, for $7.2 million at about two cents per acre .
Suburbs	Suburbs, usually referring to a residential area, are defined in various different ways around the world. They can be the residential areas of a large city, or separate residential communities within commuting distance of a city. Some Suburbs have a degree of political autonomy, and most have lower population density than inner city neighborhoods.
Forced migration	Forced migration refers to the coerced movement of a person or persons away from their home or home region. It often connotes violent coercion, and is used interchangeably with the terms `displacement` or forced displacement. A specific form of Forced migration is population transfer, which is a coherent policy to move unwanted persons, perhaps as an attempt at `ethnic cleansing`.
Triangular trade	Triangular trade is an historical term indicating trade among three ports or regions. Triangular trade usually evolves when a region has export commodities that are not required in the region from which its major imports come. Triangular trade thus provides a mechanism for rectifying trade imbalances between these regions.
Diffusion	`Diffusion` is a time-dependent process , constituted by random motion of given entities and causing the statistical distribution of these entities to spread in space. The concept of Diffusion is tied to notion of mass transport, driven by a concentration gradient. The concept of Diffusion emerged in the physical sciences.

Slavery	Slavery is a form of forced labour in which people are considered to be the property of others. Slaves can be held against their will from the time of their capture, purchase or birth, and deprived of the right to leave, to refuse to work, or to receive compensation (such as wages).
	With around 27 million people, there are more slaves in the world today than at any point in history, more than twice as many as all the African slaves brought to the Americas.
World War I	World War I was a military conflict that lasted from 1914 to 1918 and involved most of the world's great powers, assembled in two opposing alliances: the Allies (centred around the Triple Entente) against the Central Powers. More than 70 million military personnel, including 60 million Europeans, were mobilised in one of the largest wars in history. More than 15 million people were killed, making it one of the deadliest conflicts in history.
World War II	World War II was the deadliest military conflict in history. Over 60 million people were killed. The tables below give a detailed country-by-country count of human losses.
Sharecropping	Sharecropping is a system of agriculture or agricultural production in which a landowner allows a tenant to use the land in return for a share of the crop produced on the land (e.g., 50 % of the crop). This should not be confused with a crop fixed rent contract, in which a landowner allows a tenant to use the land in return for a fixed amount of crop per unit of land (e.g., 1 T/ha). Sharecropping(1865-1877).
Ghetto	Originally used in Venice to describe the area where Jews were compelled to live, a Ghetto is now described as a `portion of a city in which members of a minority group live; especially because of social, legal, or economic pressure.`
	The word `Ghetto` actually comes from the word `getto` or `gheto`, which means slag in Venetian, and was used in this sense in a reference to a foundry where slag was stored located on the same island as the area of Jewish confinement. An alternative etymology is from Italian borGhetto, diminutive of borgo `borough`.
	The corresponding German term was Judengasse known as the Jewish Quarter.
Brown v. Board of Education of Topeka	Brown v. Board of Education of Topeka, 347 U.S. 483 (1954), was a landmark decision of the United States Supreme Court that declared state laws establishing separate public schools for black and white students denied black children equal educational opportunities. The decision overturned earlier rulings going back to Plessy v. Ferguson in 1896. Handed down on May 17, 1954, the Warren Court's unanimous (9-0) decision stated that `separate educational facilities are inherently unequal.` As a result, de jure racial segregation was ruled a violation of the Equal Protection Clause of the Fourteenth Amendment of the United States Constitution. This victory paved the way for integration and the civil rights movement.
Genocide	Genocide is the deliberate and systematic destruction, in whole or in part, of an ethnic, racial, religious, a legal definition is found in the 1948 United Nations Convention on the Prevention and Punishment of the Crime of Genocide (CPPCG`

The preamble to the CPPCG states that instances of Genocide have taken place throughout history, but it was not until Raphael Lemkin coined the term and the prosecution of perpetrators of the Holocaust at the Nuremberg trials that the United Nations agreed to the CPPCG which defined the crime of Genocide under international law.

White flight

White flight is the sociologic and demographic term denoting the trend wherein white people flee desegregated urban communities, and move to other places like commuter towns; although an American coinage, `White flight` denotes like behavior in other countries. In the U.S. the Brown v. Board of Education (1954) decision of the Supreme Court -- ordering the de jure racial desegregation of public schools in the United States -- was and remains a major factor propelling White flight from mixed-race cities.

The business practices of redlining, mortgage discrimination, and racially-restrictive covenants accelerated White flight to the suburbs.

Ireland

Ireland ; Ulster Scots: Airlann, Latin: Hibernia) is the third-largest island in Europe and the twentieth-largest island in the world. It lies to the north-west of continental Europe and is surrounded by hundreds of islands and islets. To the east of Ireland, separated by the Irish Sea, is the island of Great Britain.

Inuit language

The Inuit language is traditionally spoken across the North American Arctic and to some extent in the subarctic in Labrador. It is also spoken in far eastern Russia, particularly the Diomede Islands, but is severely endangered in Russia today and is spoken only in a few villages on the Chukchi Peninsula. The Inuit live primarily in three countries: Greenland , Canada (specifically the Nunatsiavut region of Labrador, the Nunavik region of Quebec, Nunavut, and the Northwest Territories), and the United States (specifically the state of Alaska).

Nationalism

Nationalism generally involves the identification of an ethnic identity with a state. The subject can include the belief that one`s nation is of primary importance. It is also used to describe a movement to establish or protect a homeland (usually an autonomous state) for an ethnic group.

Nation

Nationalism appeared in Africa and Asia after World War I, led by politicians like Mustafa Kemal Atatürk. But only after World War II did its influence really become apparent in political processes, especially in the formation of states as a result of decolonization.

In 1945, when the United Nations were founded, eight of its members were Asian states, and four, African.

Nation state	The origins and early history of nation-states are disputed. A major theoretical issue is: `which came first-- the nation or the Nation state?` For nationalists themselves, the answer is that the nation existed first, nationalist movements arose to present its legitimate demand for sovereignty, and the nation-state met that demand. Some `modernisation theories` of nationalism see the national identity largely as a product of government policy, to unify and modernise an already existing state.
Boundaries	Boundaries--particularly field Boundaries--are among the oldest features in an English rural landscape. Although a boundary itself is an abstract concept, the boundary can often be seen by differences in land use on either side.
	Many field Boundaries in the central region of England originated with the enclosure of the previous open fields in the 18th or 19th centuries.
Communism	Communism is a social structure in which classes are abolished and property is commonly controlled, as well as a political philosophy and social movement that advocates and aims to create such a society. Karl Marx, the father of communist thought, posited that communism would be the final stage in society, which would be achieved through a proletarian revolution and only possible after a socialist stage develops the productive forces, leading to a superabundance of goods and services.
	`Pure communism` in the Marxian sense refers to a classless, stateless and oppression-free society where decisions on what to produce and what policies to pursue are made democratically, allowing every member of society to participate in the decision-making process in both the political and economic spheres of life.
Socialist realism	Socialist realism is a style of realistic art which developed under Communism in the Soviet Union and became a dominant style in other communist countries. Socialist realism is teleologically-oriented style which has as its purpose the furtherance of the goals of socialism and communism. Although related, it should not be confused with Social realism a type of art that realistically depicts subjects of social concern.
Somalia	Somalia , officially the Republic of Somalia and formerly known as the Somali Democratic Republic, is a country located in the Horn of Africa. It is bordered by Djibouti to the northwest, Kenya to the southwest, the Gulf of Aden with Yemen to the north, the Indian Ocean to the east, and Ethiopia to the west.
	In antiquity, Somalia was an important center for commerce with the rest of the ancient world. Its sailors and merchants were the main suppliers of frankincense, myrrh and spices, items which were considered valuable luxuries by the Ancient Egyptians, Phoenicians, Mycenaeans and Babylonians with whom the Somali people traded.

South Asia	South Asia is the southern region of the Asian continent, which comprises the sub-Himalayan countries and, for some authorities , also includes the adjoining countries on the west and the east. Topographically, it is dominated by the Indian Plate, which rises above sea level as the Indian subcontinent south of the Himalayas and the Hindu Kush. South Asia is surrounded by Western Asia, Central Asia, Eastern Asia, Southeastern Asia and the Indian ocean.
Ethnic cleansing	Ethnic cleansing is a term that has come to be used broadly to describe all forms of ethnically-motivated violence, ranging from murder, rape, and torture to the forcible removal of populations. A 1993 United Nations Commission defined it more specifically as, `the planned deliberate removal from a specific territory, persons of a particular ethnic group, by force or intimidation, in order to render that area ethnically homogenous.` The term entered English and international media usage in the early 1990s to describe war events in the former Yugoslavia. The term Ethnic cleansing is not to be confused with genocide.
Croatia	Croatia , officially the Republic of Croatia is a country in central and southeastern Europe, at the crossroads of the Pannonian Plain, the Balkans, and the Mediterranean Sea. Its capital (and largest city) is Zagreb. Croatia borders Slovenia and Hungary to the north, Bosnia and Herzegovina to the southeast, and Serbia and Montenegro to the east.
Herzegovina	Herzegovina is the southern region of Bosnia-Herzegovina, comprising 11,419 sq km or around 22% of the total area of the present-day country. In other sources it comprises 12,276 sq km, this constitutes 24% of Bosnia and Herzegovina. There is no official border distinguishing it from the Bosnian region, though it is generally accepted that the borders of the region are Croatia to the west, Montenegro to the south, the canton boundaries of the Herzegovina-Neretva Canton in the east and Gornji Vakuf-Uskoplje in the north.
Balkanization	Balkanization or balkanisation is a geopolitical term originally used to describe the process of fragmentation or division of a region or state into smaller regions or states that are often hostile or non-cooperative with each other. The term has arisen from the conflicts in the 20th century Balkans. While what is now termed Balkanization has occurred throughout history, the term originally described the creation of smaller, ethnically diverse states following the breakup of the Ottoman Empire after World War I. The term is also used to describe other forms of disintegration, including, for instance, the subdivision of the Internet into separate enclaves, the division of subfields and the creation of new fields from sociology, and the breakdown of cooperative arrangements due to the rise of independent competitive entities engaged in `beggar thy neighbour` bidding wars.

Political geography	Political geography is the field of human geography that is concerned with the study of both the spatially uneven outcomes of political processes and the ways in which political processes are themselves affected by spatial structures. Conventionally Political geography adopts a three scale structure for the purposes of analysis with the study of the state at the centre, above this is the study of international relations (or geopolitics), and below it is the study of localities. The primary concerns of the sub-discipline can be summarised as the inter-relationships between people, state, and territory.

Superpower	A Superpower is a state with a leading position in the international system and the ability to influence events and its own interests and project power on a worldwide scale to protect those interests; it is traditionally considered to be one step higher than a great power.

Alice Lyman Miller (Professor of National Security Affairs at the Naval Postgraduate School), defines a Superpower as `a country that has the capacity to project dominating power and influence anywhere in the world, and sometimes, in more than one region of the globe at a time, and so may plausibly attain the status of global hegemon.`

It was a term first applied in 1944 to the United States, the Soviet Union, and the British Empire. Following World War II, as the British Empire transformed itself into the Commonwealth and its territories became independent, the Soviet Union and the United States generally came to be regarded as the only two Superpowers, and confronted each other in the Cold War. |
| World War I | World War I was a military conflict that lasted from 1914 to 1918 and involved most of the world`s great powers, assembled in two opposing alliances: the Allies (centred around the Triple Entente) against the Central Powers. More than 70 million military personnel, including 60 million Europeans, were mobilised in one of the largest wars in history. More than 15 million people were killed, making it one of the deadliest conflicts in history. |
| Border | Borders define geographic boundaries of political entities or legal jurisdictions, such as governments, states or subnational administrative divisions. They may foster the setting up of buffer zones. Some Borders are fully or partially controlled, and may be crossed legally only at designated Border checkpoints. |

Boundaries	Boundaries--particularly field Boundaries--are among the oldest features in an English rural landscape. Although a boundary itself is an abstract concept, the boundary can often be seen by differences in land use on either side.
	Many field Boundaries in the central region of England originated with the enclosure of the previous open fields in the 18th or 19th centuries.
Korea	Korea (Korean: í•œêµ or í¡°ì„) is a civilization and formerly unified nation currently divided into two states. Located on the Korean Peninsula, it borders China to the northwest, Russia to the northeast, and is separated from Japan to the east by the Korea Strait.
	Korea was united until 1948; at that time it was split into South Korea and North Korea.
Nation	Nationalism appeared in Africa and Asia after World War I, led by politicians like Mustafa Kemal Atatürk. But only after World War II did its influence really become apparent in political processes, especially in the formation of states as a result of decolonization.
	In 1945, when the United Nations were founded, eight of its members were Asian states, and four, African.
Sovereignty	Sovereignty is the quality of having supreme, independent authority over a territory. It can be found in a power to rule and make law that rests on a political fact for which no purely legal explanation can be provided. The concept has been discussed, debated and questioned throughout history, from the time of the Romans through to the present day, although it has changed in its definition, concept, and application throughout, especially during the Age of Enlightenment.
Ceuta	Ceuta is an autonomous city of Spain located on the North African side of the Strait of Gibraltar, on the Mediterranean, which separates it from the Spanish mainland. The area of Ceuta is approximately 19 square kilometres .
	Ceuta is dominated by a hill called Monte Hacho, on which there is a fort used by the Spanish army.
Melilla	Melilla (Tarifit: Tamelilt/Mritch, meaning `the white one`) is an autonomous Spanish city located on the Mediterranean, on the north coast of North Africa. It was regarded as a part of Málaga province prior to 14 March 1995, when the city`s Statute of Autonomy was passed.
	Melilla was a free port before Spain joined the European Union. As of 2008 it has a population of 71,448. Its population consists of Christians, Muslims , and small minorities of Jews and Hindus.

Antarctica	Antarctica , is Earth`s southernmost continent, underlying the South Pole. It is situated in the Antarctic region of the southern hemisphere, almost entirely south of the Antarctic Circle, and is surrounded by the Southern Ocean. At 14.0 million km^2 (5.4 million sq mi), it is the fifth-largest continent in area after Asia, Africa, North America, and South America. About 98% of Antarctica is covered by ice, which averages at least 1.6 kilometres (1.0 mi) in thickness.
Antigua	Antigua is an island in the West Indies, in the Leeward Islands in the Caribbean region, the main island of the country of Antigua and Barbuda. Antigua means `ancient` in Spanish and was named by Christopher Columbus after a church in Spain, Santa Maria La Antigua -- St. Mary the Ancient. It is also known as Wadadli, from the original Amerindian inhabitants, and means approximately `our own`.
Fertile Crescent	The Fertile Crescent is a region in Western Asia It includes the comparatively fertile regions of the Levant and Mesopotamia, delimited by the dry climate of the Syrian Desert to the south and the Anatolian highlands to the north. The region is considered the cradle of civilization and saw the development of the earliest human civilizations and is the birthplace of writing and the wheel.
	The term `Fertile Crescent` was coined by University of Chicago archaeologist James Henry Breasted in his `Ancient Records of Egypt`, around 1900. The region was named so due to its rich soil and crescent shape.
Mesopotamia	Mesopotamia is a toponym for the area of the Tigris-Euphrates river system, along the Tigris and Euphrates rivers, largely corresponding to modern Iraq, as well as some parts of northeastern Syria, some parts of southeastern Turkey, and some parts of the KhÅ«zestÄ☐n Province of southwestern Iran.
	Widely considered as the cradle of civilization, Bronze Age Mesopotamia included Sumer, Akkadian, Babylonian and Assyrian empires. In the Iron Age, it was ruled by the Neo-Assyrian Empire and Neo-Babylonian Empire, and later conquered by the Achaemenid Empire.

San Marino	On the European continent(dark grey) -- [Legend]
Capital	City of San Marino 43°56′N 12°27′E / 43.933°N 12.45°E
Largest city	Dogana
Official languages	Italian[1]
Demonym	Sammarinese
Government	Parliamentary republic
- Captains Regent	Stefano Palmieri Francesco Mussoni
Establishment	
- independence from the Roman Empire	3 September 301 (traditional)
- Constitution	8 October 1600
Area	
- Total	61.2 km² (220th) 23.5 sq mi
- Water (%)	negligible
Population	
- July 2008 estimate	29,973 (209th)
- Density	489/km² (20th) 1,225/sq mi
GDP (PPP)	2007 estimate
- Total	$1662 million (195th)
- Per capita	$55,449 (6th)
HDI (2003)	n/a (unranked) (n/a)
Currency	Euro (â‚¬) (EUR)
Time zone	CET (UTC+1)
- Summer (DST)	CEST (UTC+2)
Drives on the	right
Internet TLD	.sm
Calling code	+378
Patron saint	St. Agatha

[1] `San Marino` (PDF). UNECE. http://www.unece.org/stats/trend/smr.pdf.

The Most Serene Republic of San Marino /ËŒsæn mÉ™ËˆriË□noÊŠ/ (helpÂ·info) (Italian: Serenissima Repubblica di San Marino) is a country situated in the Apennine Mountains.

The	The word the is the only definite article in the English language, and the most frequently used word in English the article the is often used as the very first part of a noun phrase in English.
Christianity	Christianity is a monotheistic religion based on the life and teachings of Jesus of Nazareth as presented in the New Testament.

Christians believe Jesus is the son of God, God having become man and the savior of humanity. Christians, therefore, commonly refer to Jesus as Christ or Messiah.

Empire

The term Empire derives from the Latin imperium. Politically, an Empire is a geographically extensive group of states and peoples united and ruled either by a monarch (emperor, empress) or an oligarchy. Geopolitically, the term Empire has denoted very different, territorially-extreme states -- at the strong end, the extensive Spanish Empire and the British Empire (19th c।), at the weak end, the Holy Roman Empire (8th c.-19th c.), in its Medieval and early-modern forms, and the Byzantine Empire (15th c)., that was a direct continuation of the Roman Empire, that, in its final century of existence, was more a city-state than a territorial Empire.

Imperialism

Imperialism, defined by the dictionary of human geography, is `the creation and maintenance of an unequal economic, cultural and territorial relationship, usually between states and often in the form of an empire, based on domination and subordination.` Imperialism, in many ways, is described as a primarily western concept that employs `expansionist - capitalist - and latterly communist - systems.`

Imperialism is considered the control by one state of other territories. Through political or military means (direct Imperialism), the imperial power may take over the government of a particular territory, or through economic processes (indirect Imperialism), in which the concerned region is officially self-governing but linked to the imperial power by, often unequal, trade relations. Furthermore, the notion of cultural Imperialism is indicated by `existing or traditional ways of life and ways of thinking [that] are subordinated to the culture of the imperialists.`

The term Imperialism commonly refers to a political or geographical domain such as the Ottoman Empire, the French Empire the Russian Empire, the Chinese Empire, or the British Empire, etc., but the term can equally be applied to domains of knowledge, beliefs, values and expertise, such as the empires of Christianity or Islam .

Sovereign state

A Sovereign state, commonly simply referred to as a state, is a political association with effective internal and external sovereignty over a geographic area and population which is not dependent on, unrecognised states will often find it hard to exercise full treaty-making powers and engage in diplomatic relations with other Sovereign states.

Although the term often includes broadly all institutions of government or rule--ancient and modern--the modern state system bears a number of characteristics that were first consolidated beginning in earnest in the 15th century, when the term `state` also acquired its current meaning.

Africa	Africa is the world's second-largest and second most-populous continent, after Asia. At about 30.2 million km^2 (11.7 million sq mi) including adjacent islands, it covers 6% of the Earth's total surface area and 20.4% of the total land area. With a billion people in 61 territories, it accounts for about 14.72% of the World's human population.
Angola	Angola, officially the Republic of Angola, is a country in south-central Africa bordered by Namibia on the south, Democratic Republic of the Congo on the north, and Zambia on the east; its west coast is on the Atlantic Ocean. The exclave province of Cabinda has a border with the Republic of the Congo and the Democratic Republic of the Congo.
	Angola was a Portuguese overseas territory from the 16th century to 1975. After independence, Angola was the scene of an intense civil war from 1975 to 2002. The country is the second-largest petroleum and diamond producer in sub-Saharan Africa; however, its life expectancy and infant mortality rates are both among the worst ranked in the world.
Cabinda	Cabinda (also spelled Kabinda) is an exclave and province of Angola, a status that has been disputed by many political organizations in the territory. The capital city is also called Cabinda. The province is divided into four municipalities - Belize, Buco Zau, Cabinda and Congo.
Caprivi Strip	Caprivi, sometimes called the Caprivi Strip or the Okavango Strip and formally known as Itenge, is a narrow protrusion of Namibia eastwards about 450 km (280 miles), between Botswana on the south, Angola and Zambia to the north, and Okavango Region to the west. Caprivi is bordered by the Okavango, Kwando, Chobe and Zambezi rivers. Its largest settlement is the town of Katima Mulilo.
Demographic	Demographics data are the characteristics of a population as used in government, marketing or opinion research). Commonly-used Demographics include sex, race, age, income, disabilities, mobility (in terms of travel time to work or number of vehicles available), educational attainment, home ownership, employment status, and even location.
Demographic transition	The Demographic transition model (DTM) is a model used to represent the process of explaining the transformation of countries from high birth rates and high death rates to low birth rates and low death rates as part of the economic development of a country from a pre-industrial to an industrialized economy. It is based on an interpretation begun in 1929 by the American demographer Warren Thompson of prior observed changes, or transitions, in birth and death rates in industrialized societies over the past two hundred years.
	Most developed countries are beyond stage three of the model; the majority of developing countries are in stage 2 or stage 3. The model was based on the changes seen in Europe so these countries follow the DTM relatively well.
Indonesia	The Republic of Indonesia is a country in Southeast Asia and Oceania. Indonesia comprises 17,508 islands. With a population of around 230 million people, it is the world's fourth most populous country, with the world's largest population of Muslims.

Landlocked	A landlocked country is commonly defined as one enclosed or nearly enclosed by land. As of 2008, there are 44 landlocked countries in the world. Of the major landmasses, only North America and Australia do not have a landlocked country inside their respective continents.
Lesotho	Lesotho , officially the Kingdom of Lesotho, is a landlocked country and enclave -- entirely surrounded by the Republic of South Africa. It is just over 30,000 km^2 in size with an estimated population of almost 1,800,000. Its capital and largest city is Maseru. Lesotho is the southernmost landlocked country in the world. It is a member of the Commonwealth of Nations.
AID	Aid is a voluntary transfer of resources from one country to another, given at least partly with the objective of benefiting the recipient country. It may have other functions as well: it may be given as a signal of diplomatic approval, or to strengthen a military ally, to reward a government for behaviour desired by the donor, to extend the donor`s cultural influence, to provide infrastructure needed by the donor for resource extraction from the recipient country, or to gain other kinds of commercial access. Humanitarianism and altruism are, nevertheless, significant motivations for the giving of Aid.
Area studies	Area studies are interdisciplinary fields of research and scholarship pertaining to particular geographical, national/federal, in the practice of scholarship, many heterogeneous fields of research, encompassing both the social sciences and the humanities. Typical Area studies programs involve history, political science, sociology, cultural studies, languages, geography, literature, and related disciplines.
Aouzou Strip	The Aouzou Strip Ù‚Ø·Ø§Ø¹¹ Ø£Ù˜Ø²Ù˜ (alternatively, Aozou Strip) is a strip of land in northern Chad which lies along the border with Libya, extending south to a depth of about 100 kilometers into Chad`s Bourkou-Ennedi-Tibesti Region. Claimed to be rich with uranium deposits, a dispute over the control of this area with Libya led to a war between the two countries. In 1973, Libya engaged in military operations in the Aouzou Strip to gain access to minerals and to use it as a base of influence in Chadian politics.
Unitary state	A Unitary state is a sovereign state governed as one single unit in which the central government is supreme and any administrative divisions (subnational units) exercise only powers that the central government chooses to delegate. Many states in the world have a unitary system of government. Unitary states are contrasted with federal states (federations): · In a Unitary state, subnational units are created and abolished and their powers may be broadened and narrowed, by the central government. Although political power in Unitary states may be delegated through devolution to local government by statute, the central government remains supreme; it may abrogate the acts of devolved governments or curtail their powers.

· The United Kingdom is an example of a Unitary state.

Communism	Communism is a social structure in which classes are abolished and property is commonly controlled, as well as a political philosophy and social movement that advocates and aims to create such a society. Karl Marx, the father of communist thought, posited that communism would be the final stage in society, which would be achieved through a proletarian revolution and only possible after a socialist stage develops the productive forces, leading to a superabundance of goods and services. `Pure communism` in the Marxian sense refers to a classless, stateless and oppression-free society where decisions on what to produce and what policies to pursue are made democratically, allowing every member of society to participate in the decision-making process in both the political and economic spheres of life.
Balance of power	In international relations, a balance of power exists when there is parity or stability between competing forces. As a term in international law for a `just equilibrium` between the members of the family of nations, it expresses the doctrine intended to prevent any one nation from becoming sufficiently strong so as to enable it to enforce its will upon the rest. `BoP` is a central concept in neorealist theory.
Crisis	A Crisis may occur on a personal or societal level. It may be an unstable and dangerous social situation, in political, social, economic, military affairs, or a large-scale environmental event, especially one involving an impending abrupt change. More loosely, it is a term meaning `a testing time` or `emergency event`.
Cuban Missile Crisis	The Cuban Missile Crisis was a confrontation between the United States, the Soviet Union, and Cuba in October 1962, during the Cold War. In Russia, former Eastern Bloc countries, and other communist countries , it is termed the `Caribbean Crisis` , while in Cuba it is called the `October Crisis` . In September 1962, the Cuban and Soviet governments placed nuclear missiles in Cuba.
Unity	UNITY is the theoretical political journal of Socialist Worker (Aotearoa), published quarterly in Auckland, New Zealand, since December 2005. It is edited by Daphne Lawless, and each issue focuses on a central theme of interest to the socialist and radical left movement. The first edition of UNITY, published in December 2005, explored the issue of Left regroupment both in New Zealand and internationally. The second edition (March 2006) looked at the history of the Labour Party, contending that traditional Social Democracy had now morphed into Social Liberalism.

Unification of Germany	The formal Unification of Germany into a politically and administratively integrated nation state officially occurred on 18 January 1871 at the Versailles Palace`s Hall of Mirrors in France. Princes of the German states gathered there to proclaim Wilhelm of Prussia as Emperor Wilhelm of the German Empire after the French capitulation in the Franco-Prussian War. Unofficially, the transition of the German-speaking states into a federated organization of states occurred over nearly a century of experimentation.
World Heritage Site	A UNESCO World Heritage Site is a site (such as a forest, mountain, lake, desert, monument, building, complex) that is on the list that is maintained by the international World Heritage Programme administered by the UNESCO World Heritage Committee, composed of 21 state parties which are elected by their General Assembly for a four-year term. A World Heritage Site is a place of either cultural or physical significance.

The program catalogues, names, and conserves sites of outstanding cultural or natural importance to the common heritage of humanity. |
| Irish Republican Army | The Irish Republican Army was an Irish republican revolutionary military organisation. It was descended from the Irish Volunteers, an organisation established on 25 November 1913 that staged the Easter Rising in April 1916. In 1919, the Irish Republic that had been proclaimed during the Easter Rising was formally established by an elected assembly (Dáil Éireann),and the Irish Volunteers were recognised by Dáil Éireann as its legitimate army. Thereafter, the Irish Republican Army waged a guerrilla campaign against British rule in Ireland in the 1919-21 Irish War of Independence. |
| Islam | Islam is the religion articulated by the Qur`an, a religious book considered by its adherents to be the verbatim word of the single incomparable God , and by the Prophet of Islam Muhammad`s demonstrations and real-life examples (called the Sunnah, collected through narration of his companions in collections of Hadith). Islam literally means submission to God .

An adherent of Islam is a Muslim, meaning `one who submits (to God)`. |
| Taliban | The Taliban is a Sunni Islamist political movement that governed Afghanistan from 1996 until they were overthrown in late 2001 during Operation Enduring Freedom. It has regrouped since 2004 and revived as a strong insurgency movement governing at the local level and fighting a guerrilla war against the governments of Afghanistan, Pakistan, and the NATO-led International Security Assistance Force (ISAF). The movement is made up of members belonging to different ethnic Pashtun tribes, along with a number of volunteers from nearby Islamic countries such as Uzbeks, Tajiks, Chechens, Arabs, Punjabis and others. |
| Desert Storm | The Persian Gulf War , commonly refered to as the Gulf War, and also known as the First Gulf War, the Second Gulf War, by Iraqi leader Saddam Hussein as The Mother of all Battles, and commonly as Desert Storm for the military response, was the final conflict, which was initiated with United Nations authorization, by a coalition force from 34 nations against Iraq, with the expressed purpose of expelling Iraqi forces from Kuwait after its invasion and annexation on 2 August 1990. |

The invasion of Kuwait by Iraqi troops that began 2 August 1990 was met with international condemnation, and brought both immediate economic sanctions against Iraq by members of the UN Security Council. U.S. President George H. W. Bush deployed American forces to Saudi Arabia and urged other countries to send their own forces to the scene.

Iran

The Islamic Republic of Iran has a comprehensive and effective program of family planning. While Iran`s population grew at a rate of more than 3%/year between 1956 and 1986, the growth rate began to decline in the late 1980s and early 1990s after the government initiated a major population control program. By 2007 the growth rate had declined to 0.7 percent per year, with a birth rate of 17 per 1,000 persons and a death rate of 6 per 1,000. Reports by the UN show birth control policies in Iran to be effective with the country topping the list of greatest fertility decreases.

Ethnic

An ethnic group is a group of humans whose members identify with each other, through a common heritage that is real or assumed. This shared heritage may be based upon putative common ancestry, history, kinship, religion, language, shared territory, nationality or physical appearance. Members of an ethnic group are conscious of belonging to an ethnic group; moreover ethnic identity is further marked by the recognition from others of a group`s distinctiveness.

Chapter 9. Development

Developed country	The term Developed country is used to describe countries that have a high level of development according to some criteria. Which criteria, and which countries are classified as being developed, is a contentious issue and there is fierce debate about this. Economic criteria have tended to dominate discussions.
Birth rate	Crude Birth rate is the nativity or childbirths per 1,000 people per year.
	According to the United Nations` World Population Prospects: The 2008 Revision Population Database, crude Birth rate is the Number of births over a given period divided by the person-years lived by the population over that period. It is expressed as number of births per 1,000 population.
Economic indicators	An economic indicator (or business indicator) is a statistic about the economy. Economic indicators(a measure for inflation), Consumer Leverage Ratio, industrial production, bankruptcies, Gross Domestic Product, broadband internet penetration, retail sales, stock market prices, money supply changes.
	The leading business cycle dating committee in the United States of America is the National Bureau of Economic Research (private).
Secondary sector	The secondary sector of the economy includes those economic sectors that create a finished, usable product: manufacturing and construction. This was the primary economic sector in America from the 1820`s-1940`s
	This sector generally takes the output of the primary sector and manufactures finished goods or where they are suitable for use by other businesses, for export, or sale to domestic consumers. This sector is often divided into light industry and heavy industry.
Tertiary sector	The tertiary sector of the economy (also known as the service sector or the service industry) is one of the three economic sectors, the others being the secondary sector (approximately manufacturing) and the primary sector (extraction such as mining, agriculture and fishing). The general definition of the tertiary sector is producing a service instead of just an end product, in the case of the secondary sector. Sometimes an additional sector, the `quaternary sector`, is defined for the sharing of information (which normally belongs to the tertiary sector)
	The tertiary sector is defined by exclusion of the two other sectors.
Brain drain	Brain drain or human capital flight is a large emigration of individuals with technical skills or knowledge, normally due to conflict, lack of opportunity, political instability, since emigrants usually take with them the fraction of value of their training sponsored by the government. It is a parallel of capital flight which refers to the same movement of financial capital.

Demographic	Demographics data are the characteristics of a population as used in government, marketing or opinion research). Commonly-used Demographics include sex, race, age, income, disabilities, mobility (in terms of travel time to work or number of vehicles available), educational attainment, home ownership, employment status, and even location.
Crude birth rate	Crude birth rate is the nativity or childbirths per 1,000 people per year. According to the United Nations` World Population Prospects: The 2008 Revision Population Database, Crude birth rate(births in a period / population of person-years over that period). According to the Dictionary of Geography by Audrey Clark, Crude birth rate is also known as natural increase.
Life expectancy	Life expectancy is the expected (in the statistical sense) number of years of life remaining at a given age. It is denoted by e_x, which means the average number of subsequent years of life for someone now aged x, according to a particular mortality experience. (In technical literature, this symbol means the average number of complete years of life remaining, ie excluding fractions of a year.
Bermuda Triangle	The Bermuda Triangle, also known as the Devil`s Triangle, is a region in the western part of the North Atlantic Ocean in which a number of aircraft and surface vessels are alleged to have mysteriously disappeared in a manner that cannot be explained by human error, piracy, equipment failure, a suspension of the laws of physics, or activity by extraterrestrial beings. A substantial body of documentation reveals, however, that a significant portion of the allegedly mysterious incidents have been inaccurately reported or embellished by later authors, and numerous official agencies have stated that the number and nature of disappearances in the region is similar to any other area of ocean.
Africa	Africa is the world`s second-largest and second most-populous continent, after Asia. At about 30.2 million $km^2$ (11.7 million sq mi) including adjacent islands, it covers 6% of the Earth`s total surface area and 20.4% of the total land area. With a billion people in 61 territories, it accounts for about 14.72% of the World`s human population.
Buddhism	Buddhism is a religion and philosophy encompassing a variety of traditions, beliefs and practices, largely based on teachings attributed to Siddhartha Gautama, commonly known as the Buddha . Buddha lived and taught in the northeastern Indian subcontinent sometime between the 6th and 4th centuries BCE. He is recognized by adherents as an awakened teacher who shared his insights to help sentient beings end suffering, achieve nirvana, and escape what is seen as a cycle of suffering and rebirth. Two major branches of Buddhism are recognized: Theravada and Mahayana (`The Great Vehicle`).

Communism	Communism is a social structure in which classes are abolished and property is commonly controlled, as well as a political philosophy and social movement that advocates and aims to create such a society. Karl Marx, the father of communist thought, posited that communism would be the final stage in society, which would be achieved through a proletarian revolution and only possible after a socialist stage develops the productive forces, leading to a superabundance of goods and services. `Pure communism` in the Marxian sense refers to a classless, stateless and oppression-free society where decisions on what to produce and what policies to pursue are made democratically, allowing every member of society to participate in the decision-making process in both the political and economic spheres of life.
Latin America	Latin America is a region of the Americas where Romance languages - particularly Spanish, Portuguese, and variably French - are primarily spoken. Latin America has an area of approximately 21,069,501 km^2 , almost 3.9% of the Earth`s surface or 14.1% of its land surface area. As of 2008, its population was estimated at more than 569 million.
Middle East	The Middle East is a region that encompasses southwestern Asia and Egypt. In some contexts, the term has recently been expanded in usage to sometimes include Pakistan and Afghanistan, the Caucacus, and North Africa. It`s often used as a synonym for Near East, in opposition to Far East. The corresponding adjective is Middle-Eastern and the derived noun is Middle-Easterner.
Southeast Asia	Southeast Asia or Southeastern Asia is a subregion of Asia, consisting of the countries that are geographically south of China and Taiwan, east of India and north of Australia. The region lies on the intersection of geological plates, with heavy seismic and volcanic activity. Southeast Asia consists of two geographic regions: the Asian mainland (aka.
The	The word the is the only definite article in the English language, and the most frequently used word in English the article the is often used as the very first part of a noun phrase in English.
South Asia	South Asia is the southern region of the Asian continent, which comprises the sub-Himalayan countries and, for some authorities , also includes the adjoining countries on the west and the east. Topographically, it is dominated by the Indian Plate, which rises above sea level as the Indian subcontinent south of the Himalayas and the Hindu Kush. South Asia is surrounded by Western Asia, Central Asia, Eastern Asia, Southeastern Asia and the Indian ocean.

Gender Empowerment Measure	The Gender Empowerment Measure is a measure of inequalities between men`s and women`s opportunities in a country. It combines inequalities in three areas: political participation and decision making, economic participation and decision making, and power over economic resources. It is one of the five indicators used by the United Nations Development Programme in its annual Human Development Report.
Genocide	Genocide is the deliberate and systematic destruction, in whole or in part, of an ethnic, racial, religious, a legal definition is found in the 1948 United Nations Convention on the Prevention and Punishment of the Crime of Genocide (CPPCG`
	The preamble to the CPPCG states that instances of Genocide have taken place throughout history, but it was not until Raphael Lemkin coined the term and the prosecution of perpetrators of the Holocaust at the Nuremberg trials that the United Nations agreed to the CPPCG which defined the crime of Genocide under international law.
International trade	International trade is exchange of capital, goods, and services across international borders or territories. It refers to exports of goods and services by a firm to a foreign-based buyer (importer) In most countries, it represents a significant share of gross domestic product (GDP). While international trade has been present throughout much of history , its economic, social, and political importance has been on the rise in recent centuries.
Korea	Korea (Korean: í•œêµ or ì¡°ì„) is a civilization and formerly unified nation currently divided into two states. Located on the Korean Peninsula, it borders China to the northwest, Russia to the northeast, and is separated from Japan to the east by the Korea Strait.
	Korea was united until 1948; at that time it was split into South Korea and North Korea.
World Bank	The World Bank is one of two institutions created at the Bretton Woods Conference in 1944. The International Monetary Fund, a related institution is the second. Delegates from many countries attended the Bretton Woods Conference. The most powerful countries in attendance were the United States and United Kingdom which dominated negotiations.
Grameen Bank	The Grameen Bank is a microfinance organization and community development bank started in Bangladesh that makes small loans (known as microcredit or `grameencredit`) to the impoverished without requiring collateral. The word `Grameen`, derived from the word `gram` or `village`, means `of the village`. The system of this bank is based on the idea that the poor have skills that are under-utilized.

Diffusion	`Diffusion` is a time-dependent process , constituted by random motion of given entities and causing the statistical distribution of these entities to spread in space. The concept of Diffusion is tied to notion of mass transport, driven by a concentration gradient. The concept of Diffusion emerged in the physical sciences.
Demographic	Demographics data are the characteristics of a population as used in government, marketing or opinion research). Commonly-used Demographics include sex, race, age, income, disabilities, mobility (in terms of travel time to work or number of vehicles available), educational attainment, home ownership, employment status, and even location.
Africa	Africa is the world`s second-largest and second most-populous continent, after Asia. At about 30.2 million km$^2$ (11.7 million sq mi) including adjacent islands, it covers 6% of the Earth`s total surface area and 20.4% of the total land area. With a billion people in 61 territories, it accounts for about 14.72% of the World`s human population.
Subsistence agriculture	Subsistence agriculture is self-sufficiency farming in which farmers grow only enough food to feed their families. The typical subsistence farm has a range of crops and animals needed by the family to eat during the year. Planting decisions are made with an eye toward what the family will need during the coming year, rather than market prices.
Middle East	The Middle East is a region that encompasses southwestern Asia and Egypt. In some contexts, the term has recently been expanded in usage to sometimes include Pakistan and Afghanistan, the Caucacus, and North Africa. It`s often used as a synonym for Near East, in opposition to Far East. The corresponding adjective is Middle-Eastern and the derived noun is Middle-Easterner.
Area studies	Area studies are interdisciplinary fields of research and scholarship pertaining to particular geographical, national/federal, in the practice of scholarship, many heterogeneous fields of research, encompassing both the social sciences and the humanities. Typical Area studies programs involve history, political science, sociology, cultural studies, languages, geography, literature, and related disciplines.
Nomadic people	Nomadic people are communities of people who move from one place to another, rather than settling permanently in one location. There are an estimated 30-40 million nomads in the world. Many cultures have traditionally been nomadic, but traditional nomadic behavior is increasingly rare in industrialized countries.
Land use	`Land use` is also often used to refer to the distinct Land use types in Zoning. Land use is the human modification of natural environment or wilderness into built environment such as fields, pastures, and settlements. The major effect of Land use on land cover since 1750 has been deforestation of temperate regions.

Slash and burn	Slash and burn consists of cutting and burning of forests or woodlands to create fields for agriculture or pasture for livestock, or for a variety of other purposes. It is sometimes part of shifting cultivation agriculture, and of transhumance livestock herding. Historically, the practice of Slash and burn has been widely practiced throughout most of the world, in grasslands as well as woodlands, and known by many names.
Central business district	A Central business district (,) is the commercial and often geographic heart of a city. In Algeria, Australia, Hong Kong , Kenya, New Zealand, Philippines, Singapore and South Africa, the phrase is commonly used, and is often colloquially abbreviated to . Ortigas Center, the 2nd most important Central business district in Metro Manila The Central business district is the central district of a city, usually typified by a concentration of retail and commercial buildings.
Forest	A Forest is an area with a high density of trees. There are many definitions of a Forest, based on the various criteria. These plant communities cover approximately 9.4% of the Earth`s surface (or 30% of total land area) in many different regions and function as habitats for organisms, hydrologic flow modulators, and soil conservers, constituting one of the most important aspects of the Earth`s biosphere.
Deforestation	Deforestation is the clearance of naturally occurring forests by the processes of humans` logging and/or burning of trees in a forested area. deforestation occurs because of many reasons: trees or derived charcoal are used as or sold for fuel or a commodity to be used by humans, while cleared land is used by humans as pasture for livestock, plantations of commodities, and settlements. People`s removal of trees without sufficient reforestation has resulted in damage to habitat, biodiversity loss and aridity.
Transhumance	Transhumance is the seasonal movement of people with their livestock over relatively short distances, typically to higher pastures in summer and to lower valleys in winter. Herders have a permanent home, typically in valleys. Only the herds travel, with the people necessary to tend them.
Farm	A Farm is an area of land, including various structures, devoted primarily to the practice of producing and managing food (produce, grains), fibers and, increasingly, fuel. It is the basic production facility in food production. Farms may be owned and operated by a single individual, family, community, corporation or a company.

Popular culture	Popular culture is the totality of ideas, perspectives, attitudes, memes, images and other phenomena that are deemed preferred per an informal consensus within the mainstream of a given culture, specifically Western culture of the early to mid 20th century and the emerging global mainstream of the late 20th to 21st century. Heavily influenced by mass media, this collection of ideas permeates the everyday lives of the society. By contrast, folklore refers to the cultural mainstream of more local or pre-industrial societies.
Truck farming	Truck farming is the cultivation of one or a few fruit or vegetable crops on a relatively large scale for transport to distant markets where the crop cannot be grown due to climate. This is contrasted to market gardening, where a variety of crops are grown on small farms for sale to local markets. Truck farms are larger, grow fewer types of crops, or only one type, and often grow seasonal crops.
The	The word the is the only definite article in the English language, and the most frequently used word in English the article the is often used as the very first part of a noun phrase in English.
International trade	International trade is exchange of capital, goods, and services across international borders or territories. It refers to exports of goods and services by a firm to a foreign-based buyer (importer) In most countries, it represents a significant share of gross domestic product (GDP). While international trade has been present throughout much of history , its economic, social, and political importance has been on the rise in recent centuries.
Population	IV class="thumb tright"> Distribution of world Population in 1994. Time taken for each billion people to be added to the world`s Population (including future estimates).
Population growth	Population growth is the change in population over time, and can be quantified as the change in the number of individuals in a population using `per unit time` for measurement. The term Population growth can technically refer to any species, but almost always refers to humans, and it is often used informally for the more specific demographic term Population growth rate , and is often used to refer specifically to the growth of the population of the world. Simple models of Population growth include the Malthusian Growth Model and the logistic model.
Crisis	A Crisis may occur on a personal or societal level. It may be an unstable and dangerous social situation, in political, social, economic, military affairs, or a large-scale environmental event, especially one involving an impending abrupt change. More loosely, it is a term meaning `a testing time` or `emergency event`.

Rural	The term Rurals is used as an expression of different Rural areas as not being homogeneously defined. Many authors involved in mental health research in Rural areas, stress the importance of steering clear of inflexible blanket definitions of Rurality (Philo, 2003), and to instead `select definitions of Rurality that are appropriate to the study being conducted` (Cloke, 1977). Cloke`s index categorises all areas of England and Wales into four criteria: extreme Rural, intermediate Rural, intermediate non-Rural and extreme non-Rural; as well as urban areas.
Maquiladora	A Maquiladora or maquila is a factory that imports materials and equipment on a duty-free and tariff-free basis for assembly or manufacturing and then re-exports the assembled product, usually back to the originating country. A maquila is also referred to as a `twin plant`, or `in-bond` industry. Currently about 1.3 million Mexicans are employed in Maquiladoras.
Emigration	Emigration is the act of leaving one`s native country or region to settle in another. It is the same as immigration but from the perspective of the country of origin. Human movement before the establishment of political boundaries or within one state, is termed migration.
Christianity	Christianity is a monotheistic religion based on the life and teachings of Jesus of Nazareth as presented in the New Testament. Christians believe Jesus is the son of God, God having become man and the savior of humanity. Christians, therefore, commonly refer to Jesus as Christ or Messiah.
Diffusion	`Diffusion` is a time-dependent process , constituted by random motion of given entities and causing the statistical distribution of these entities to spread in space. The concept of Diffusion is tied to notion of mass transport, driven by a concentration gradient. The concept of Diffusion emerged in the physical sciences.
Family planning	Family planning is the planning of when to have children, and the use of birth control and other techniques to implement such plans. Other techniques commonly used include sexuality education, prevention and management of sexually transmitted infections, pre-conception counseling and management, and infertility management. Family planning is sometimes used as a synonym for the use of birth control, though it often includes more.
Industrial region	Industrial region or industrial area refers to a region with extremely dense industry. It is usually heavily urbanized. Industrial regions by country:

Go to **Cram101.com** for Interactive Practice Exams for this book or virtually any of your books for $4.95/month.
And, **NEVER** highlight a book again!

125

· ABCD Region, sometimes called ABC (ABC paulista or Região do Grande ABC in Portuguese) is an Industrial region made up of seven municipalities with the greater metropolitan area of São Paulo, Brazil.

· Wagle estate, Thane

· ChÅ«kyÅ☐ Industrial Area
· Hanshin Industrial region

· KaesÅ☐ng Industrial region, North Korea
· Southeastern Maritime Industrial region, South Korea

· BiaÅ‚ystok Industrial region
· Bielsko Industrial region
· Bydgoszcz-ToruÅ„ Industrial region
· Carpathian Industrial region
· Central Industrial region
· CzÄ™stochowa Industrial region
· GdaÅ„sk Industrial region
· Upper Silesian Industrial region
· Jaworzno-Chrzanów Industrial region
· Kalisz-Ostrów Industrial region
· Kraków Industrial region
· Legnica-GÅ‚ogów Copper Area
· Lublin Industrial region
· Å□ódÅº Industrial region
· Olsztyn Industrial region
· Opole Industrial region
· Piotrków-BeÅ‚chatów Industrial region
· PoznaÅ„ Industrial region
· Rybnik Coal Area
· Old-Polish Industrial region
· Sudetian Industrial region
· Szczecin Industrial region
· Tarnobrzeg Industrial region
· Tarnów-Rzeszów Industrial region
· Warsaw Industrial region
· WrocÅ‚aw Industrial region
· Zielona Góra-Å»ary Industrial region .

Buddhism	Buddhism is a religion and philosophy encompassing a variety of traditions, beliefs and practices, largely based on teachings attributed to Siddhartha Gautama, commonly known as the Buddha . Buddha lived and taught in the northeastern Indian subcontinent sometime between the 6th and 4th centuries BCE. He is recognized by adherents as an awakened teacher who shared his insights to help sentient beings end suffering, achieve nirvana, and escape what is seen as a cycle of suffering and rebirth.

Two major branches of Buddhism are recognized: Theravada and Mahayana (`The Great Vehicle`). |
| Silesia | Silesia ; Czech: Slezsko; Silesian: ÅšlÅ¯nsk [É•lonsk]; Latin: Silesia) is a historical region of Central Europe located mostly in present-day Poland, with parts in the Czech Republic and Germany. |

Silesia is rich in mineral and natural resources, and includes several important industrial areas. Silesia's largest cities are WrocÅ‚aw, its historical capital, and Katowice in Poland, and Ostrava in the Czech Republic.

Abraham	Abraham is the founding patriarch of the Israelites, Ishmaelites, Edomite, and the Midianites and kindred peoples, according to the book of Genesis. In the absence of extra-biblical evidence for his existence, influential scholars have long questioned the historicity of his narratives. Judaism, Christianity, and Islam are sometimes referred to as the `Abrahamic religions` because of the progenitor role Abraham plays in their holy books.
Alexandria	Alexandria , with a population of 4.1 million, is the second-largest city in Egypt, and is the country's largest seaport, serving about 80% of Egypt's imports and exports. Alexandria is also an important tourist resort. Alexandria extends about 32 km along the coast of the Mediterranean Sea in north-central Egypt.
Lake	A Lake is a terrain feature , a body of liquid on the surface of a world that is localized to the bottom of basin (another type of landform or terrain feature; that is, it is not global) and moves slowly if it moves at all. Another definition is, a body of fresh or salt water of considerable size that is surrounded by land. On Earth, a body of water is considered a Lake when it is inland, not part of the ocean, is larger and deeper than a pond, and is fed by a river.
Demographic	Demographics data are the characteristics of a population as used in government, marketing or opinion research). Commonly-used Demographics include sex, race, age, income, disabilities, mobility (in terms of travel time to work or number of vehicles available), educational attainment, home ownership, employment status, and even location.
Demographic transition	The Demographic transition model (DTM) is a model used to represent the process of explaining the transformation of countries from high birth rates and high death rates to low birth rates and low death rates as part of the economic development of a country from a pre-industrial to an industrialized economy. It is based on an interpretation begun in 1929 by the American demographer Warren Thompson of prior observed changes, or transitions, in birth and death rates in industrialized societies over the past two hundred years. Most developed countries are beyond stage three of the model; the majority of developing countries are in stage 2 or stage 3. The model was based on the changes seen in Europe so these countries follow the DTM relatively well.

Africa	Africa is the world`s second-largest and second most-populous continent, after Asia. At about 30.2 million km$^2$ (11.7 million sq mi) including adjacent islands, it covers 6% of the Earth`s total surface area and 20.4% of the total land area. With a billion people in 61 territories, it accounts for about 14.72% of the World`s human population.

Capital	Flag
Capital Language(s) Political structure Governor - 1640 - 1794-1796 Historical era - Dutch annexation of Colombo - British annexation of Colombo	Colombo Dutch Colony Willem Jacobsz Coster (First) J.G. van Angelbeek (Last) Imperialism 12 May 1656 16 Feb 1796

This is a term used synonymously for the period, and the area of Ceylon or Sri Lanka that was controlled by the Dutch from 1685-1798 and their rule.

In the 1600s, Sri Lanka was partly ruled by the Portuguese invaders and the Sinhala Kingdom, who were constantly battling each other. Although the Portuguese were not winning the war, their rule was rather burdensome to the people of those areas controlled by them.

Southeast Asia	Southeast Asia or Southeastern Asia is a subregion of Asia, consisting of the countries that are geographically south of China and Taiwan, east of India and north of Australia. The region lies on the intersection of geological plates, with heavy seismic and volcanic activity. Southeast Asia consists of two geographic regions: the Asian mainland (aka.

North American Free Trade Agreement	The North American Free Trade Agreement is an agreement signed by the governments of the United States, Canada, and Mexico creating a trilateral trade bloc in North America. The agreement came into force on January 1, 1994. It superseded the Canada-United States Free Trade Agreement between the U.S. and Canada. In terms of combined purchasing power parity GDP of its members, as of 2007 the trade block is the largest in the world and second largest by nominal GDP comparison. The North American Free Trade Agreement has two supplements, the North American Agreement on Environmental Cooperation (NAAEC) and the North American Agreement on Labor Cooperation (NAALC).

Division of Labor | Division of labor or economic specialization is the specialization of cooperative labor in specific, circumscribed tasks and roles, intended to increase the productivity of labor. Historically the growth of a more and more complex Division of labor(an intellectual challenge for researchers), although the ILO and national statistical offices can provide plenty of data on request for those who wish to try.

In one study, Deon Filmer estimated that 2,474 million people participated in the global non-domestic labor force in the mid-1990s. Of these,

· around 15%, or 379 million people, worked in industry,
· a third, or 800 million worked in services, and
· over 40%, or 1,074 million, in agriculture.

Urban	Urban: An Urban area is an area with an increased density of human-created structures in comparison to the areas surrounding it. Urban areas are extremely dense population areas. An Urban area is more frequently called a city or metropolitan area.
Communism	Communism is a social structure in which classes are abolished and property is commonly controlled, as well as a political philosophy and social movement that advocates and aims to create such a society. Karl Marx, the father of communist thought, posited that communism would be the final stage in society, which would be achieved through a proletarian revolution and only possible after a socialist stage develops the productive forces, leading to a superabundance of goods and services.
	`Pure communism` in the Marxian sense refers to a classless, stateless and oppression-free society where decisions on what to produce and what policies to pursue are made democratically, allowing every member of society to participate in the decision-making process in both the political and economic spheres of life.
Linear village	In geography, a Linear village, is a small to medium-sized settlement that is formed around a transport route, such as a road, river, or canal. Initially the houses were all built on one side of the route. Wraysbury, a village in Berkshire, is one of the longest villages in England.
Rural	The term Rurals is used as an expression of different Rural areas as not being homogeneously defined. Many authors involved in mental health research in Rural areas, stress the importance of steering clear of inflexible blanket definitions of Rurality (Philo, 2003), and to instead `select definitions of Rurality that are appropriate to the study being conducted` (Cloke, 1977).
	Cloke`s index categorises all areas of England and Wales into four criteria: extreme Rural, intermediate Rural, intermediate non-Rural and extreme non-Rural; as well as urban areas.
Central place theory	Central place theory is a geographical theory that seeks to explain the number, size and location of human settlements in an urban system. The theory was created by the German geographer Walter Christaller, who asserted that settlements simply functioned as `central places` providing services to surrounding areas.
	To develop the theory, Christaller made the following simplifying assumptions:

· an isotropic , homogeneous, unbounded limitless surface (abstract space)
· an evenly distributed population
· evenly distributed resources
· all consumers have a similar purchasing power and demand for goods and services
· Consumers visit the nearest central places that provide the function which they demand.They minimize the distance to be travelled
· no provider of goods or services is able to earn excess profit(each supplier has a monopoly over a hinterland)

Therefore the trade areas of these central places who provide a particular good or service must all be of equal size

· there is only one type of transport and this would be equally easy in all directions
· transport cost is proportional to distance traveled in example, the longer the distance traveled, the higher the transport cost

The theory then relied on two concepts: threshold and range.

· Threshold is the minimum market (population or income) needed to bring about the selling of a particular good or service.
· Range is the maximum distance consumers are prepared to travel to acquire goods - at some point the cost or inconvenience will outweigh the need for the good.

The result of these consumer preferences is that a system of centers of various sizes will emerge.

Gravity model	Gravity models are used in various social sciences to predict and describe certain behaviors that mimic gravitational interaction as described in Isaac Newton`s law of gravity. Generally, the social science models contain some elements of mass and distance, which lends them to the metaphor of physical gravity.
Middle East	The Middle East is a region that encompasses southwestern Asia and Egypt. In some contexts, the term has recently been expanded in usage to sometimes include Pakistan and Afghanistan, the Caucacus, and North Africa. It`s often used as a synonym for Near East, in opposition to Far East. The corresponding adjective is Middle-Eastern and the derived noun is Middle-Easterner.

World Heritage Site	A UNESCO World Heritage Site is a site (such as a forest, mountain, lake, desert, monument, building, complex) that is on the list that is maintained by the international World Heritage Programme administered by the UNESCO World Heritage Committee, composed of 21 state parties which are elected by their General Assembly for a four-year term. A World Heritage Site is a place of either cultural or physical significance. The program catalogues, names, and conserves sites of outstanding cultural or natural importance to the common heritage of humanity.
Suburbs	Suburbs, usually referring to a residential area, are defined in various different ways around the world. They can be the residential areas of a large city, or separate residential communities within commuting distance of a city. Some Suburbs have a degree of political autonomy, and most have lower population density than inner city neighborhoods.
Rome	Rome is the capital of Italy and the country's largest and most populated municipality , with over 2.7 million residents in 1,285.3 km^2 (496.3 sq mi), while the population of the urban area is estimated by Eurostat to be 3.46 million. The metropolitan area of Rome is estimated by OECD to have a population of 3.7 million. It is located in the central-western portion of the Italian Peninsula, on the Tiber river within the Lazio region of Italy.
Empire	The term Empire derives from the Latin imperium. Politically, an Empire is a geographically extensive group of states and peoples united and ruled either by a monarch (emperor, empress) or an oligarchy. Geopolitically, the term Empire has denoted very different, territorially-extreme states -- at the strong end, the extensive Spanish Empire and the British Empire (19th c)., at the weak end, the Holy Roman Empire (8th c.-19th c)., in its Medieval and early-modern forms, and the Byzantine Empire (15th c)., that was a direct continuation of the Roman Empire, that, in its final century of existence, was more a city-state than a territorial Empire.
Central business district	A Central business district (,) is the commercial and often geographic heart of a city. In Algeria, Australia, Hong Kong , Kenya, New Zealand, Philippines, Singapore and South Africa, the phrase is commonly used, and is often colloquially abbreviated to . Ortigas Center, the 2nd most important Central business district in Metro Manila The Central business district is the central district of a city, usually typified by a concentration of retail and commercial buildings.
Land use	`Land use` is also often used to refer to the distinct Land use types in Zoning. Land use is the human modification of natural environment or wilderness into built environment such as fields, pastures, and settlements. The major effect of Land use on land cover since 1750 has been deforestation of temperate regions.
Christianity	Christianity is a monotheistic religion based on the life and teachings of Jesus of Nazareth as presented in the New Testament.

Christians believe Jesus is the son of God, God having become man and the savior of humanity. Christians, therefore, commonly refer to Jesus as Christ or Messiah.

Suburbanization	Suburbanization (or suburbanisation) is a term used to describe the growth of areas on the fringes of major cities. It is one of the many causes of the increase in urban sprawl. Many residents of metropolitan areas no longer live and work within the central urban area, choosing instead to live in satellite communities called suburbs and commute to work via automobile or mass transit.
Daily urban system	The Daily urban system is the area around a city, in which daily commuting occurs. Urban sprawl is the result of an expansion of the Daily urban system. `.

101

Suburbs	Suburbs, usually referring to a residential area, are defined in various different ways around the world. They can be the residential areas of a large city, or separate residential communities within commuting distance of a city. Some Suburbs have a degree of political autonomy, and most have lower population density than inner city neighborhoods.
Urban	Urban: An Urban area is an area with an increased density of human-created structures in comparison to the areas surrounding it. Urban areas are extremely dense population areas. An Urban area is more frequently called a city or metropolitan area.
Urbanization	Urbanization (also spelled `urbanisation`) is the physical growth of urban areas as a result of global change. Urbanization is also defined by the United Nations as movement of people from rural to urban areas with population growth equating to urban migration. The United Nations has projected that half of the world`s population would live in urban areas at the end of 2008. Urbanization is closely linked to modernization, industrialization, and the sociological process of rationalization.
Air pollution	Air pollution is the introduction of chemicals, particulate matter, or biological materials that cause harm or discomfort to humans or other living organisms, or damages the natural environment, into the atmosphere. The atmosphere is a complex, dynamic natural gaseous system that is essential to support life on planet Earth. Stratospheric ozone depletion due to Air pollution has long been recognized as a threat to human health as well as to the Earth`s ecosystems.
Population	IV class="thumb tright"> Distribution of world Population in 1994. Time taken for each billion people to be added to the world`s Population (including future estimates).
Population growth	Population growth is the change in population over time, and can be quantified as the change in the number of individuals in a population using `per unit time` for measurement. The term Population growth can technically refer to any species, but almost always refers to humans, and it is often used informally for the more specific demographic term Population growth rate , and is often used to refer specifically to the growth of the population of the world. Simple models of Population growth include the Malthusian Growth Model and the logistic model.
World Heritage Site	A UNESCO World Heritage Site is a site (such as a forest, mountain, lake, desert, monument, building, complex) that is on the list that is maintained by the international World Heritage Programme administered by the UNESCO World Heritage Committee, composed of 21 state parties which are elected by their General Assembly for a four-year term. A World Heritage Site is a place of either cultural or physical significance.

The program catalogues, names, and conserves sites of outstanding cultural or natural importance to the common heritage of humanity.

Rural

The term Rurals is used as an expression of different Rural areas as not being homogeneously defined. Many authors involved in mental health research in Rural areas, stress the importance of steering clear of inflexible blanket definitions of Rurality (Philo, 2003), and to instead `select definitions of Rurality that are appropriate to the study being conducted` (Cloke, 1977).

Cloke`s index categorises all areas of England and Wales into four criteria: extreme Rural, intermediate Rural, intermediate non-Rural and extreme non-Rural; as well as urban areas.

Concentric ring model

The Concentric ring model also known as the Burgess model is one of the earliest theoretical models to explain urban social structures. It was created by sociologist Ernest Burgess in 1925.

Based on human ecology theories done by Burgess and applied on Chicago, it was the first to give the explanation of distribution of social groups within urban areas. This Concentric ring model depicts urban land use in concentric rings: the Central Business District (or CBD) was in the middle of the model, and the city expanded in rings with different land uses.

Multiple nuclei model

The Multiple nuclei model is an ecological model put forth by Chauncy Harris and Edward Ullman in the 1945 article `The Nature of Cities.` The model describes the layout of a city. It notes that while a city may have started with a central business district, similar industries with common land-use and financial requirements are established near each other. These groupings influence their immediate neighborhood.

Sector model

The Sector model also known as the Hoyt model is a model of urban land use proposed in 1939 by economist Homer Hoyt. It is a modification of the concentric zone model of city development. The benefits of the application of this model include the fact it allows for an outward progression of growth.

Christianity

Christianity is a monotheistic religion based on the life and teachings of Jesus of Nazareth as presented in the New Testament.

Christians believe Jesus is the son of God, God having become man and the savior of humanity. Christians, therefore, commonly refer to Jesus as Christ or Messiah.

Central business district

A Central business district (,) is the commercial and often geographic heart of a city. In Algeria, Australia, Hong Kong , Kenya, New Zealand, Philippines, Singapore and South Africa, the phrase is commonly used, and is often colloquially abbreviated to .

Ortigas Center, the 2nd most important Central business district in Metro Manila

The Central business district is the central district of a city, usually typified by a concentration of retail and commercial buildings.

Post-colonial

Postcolonialism (postcolonial theory, post-colonial theory) is a specifically post-modern intellectual discourse that holds together a set of theories found among the texts and sub-texts of philosophy, film, political science, human geography and literature. These theories are reactions to the cultural legacy of colonialism.

The critical nature of postcolonial theory entails destabilizing Western way of thinking, therefore creating space for the subaltern to speak and produce alternatives to dominant discourse.

Southeast Asia

Southeast Asia or Southeastern Asia is a subregion of Asia, consisting of the countries that are geographically south of China and Taiwan, east of India and north of Australia. The region lies on the intersection of geological plates, with heavy seismic and volcanic activity.

Southeast Asia consists of two geographic regions: the Asian mainland (aka.

Urban renewal

Urban renewal is a program of land redevelopment in areas of moderate to high density urban land use. Its modern incarnation began in the late 19th century in developed nations and experienced an intense phase in the late 1940s - under the rubric of reconstruction. The process has had a major impact on many urban landscapes, and has played an important role in the history and demographics of cities around the world.

Gentrification

Gentrification and urban Gentrification denote the socio-cultural changes in an area resulting from wealthier people buying housing property in a less prosperous community. Consequent to Gentrification, the average income increases and average family size decreases in the community, which may result in the informal economic eviction of the lower-income residents, because of increased rents, house prices, and property taxes. This type of population change reduces industrial land use when it is redeveloped for commerce and housing.

Underclass

The term Underclass is a coinage which functions as a morally neutral equivalent for what was known in the eighteenth and nineteenth centuries as the `undeserving poor`. The earliest significant exponent of the term was the American sociologist and anthropologist Oscar Lewis in 1961. The Underclass, according to Lewis, has `a strong present-time orientation, with little ability to delay gratification and plan for the future` (p. xxvi).

Culture of poverty

The culture of poverty concept is a social theory explaining the cycle of poverty. Based on the concept that the poor have a unique value system, the culture of poverty theory suggests the poor remain in poverty because of their adaptations to the burdens of poverty.

The term `subculture of poverty` (later shortened to `culture of poverty`) made its first prominent appearance in the ethnography Five Families: Mexican Case Studies in the culture of poverty by anthropologist Oscar Lewis.

Annexation	Annexation is the legal incorporation of some territory into another geo-political entity . Usually, it is implied that the territory and population being annexed is the smaller, more peripheral, and weaker of the two merging entities. It can also imply a certain measure of coercion, expansionism or unilateralism on the part of the stronger of the merging entities.
Ethnic	An ethnic group is a group of humans whose members identify with each other, through a common heritage that is real or assumed. This shared heritage may be based upon putative common ancestry, history, kinship, religion, language, shared territory, nationality or physical appearance. Members of an ethnic group are conscious of belonging to an ethnic group; moreover ethnic identity is further marked by the recognition from others of a group`s distinctiveness.
Racial segregation	Racial segregation is the separation of different racial groups in daily life, such as eating in a restaurant, drinking from a water fountain, using a washroom, attending school, going to the movies, e.g).
Birth rate	Crude Birth rate is the nativity or childbirths per 1,000 people per year. According to the United Nations` World Population Prospects: The 2008 Revision Population Database, crude Birth rate is the Number of births over a given period divided by the person-years lived by the population over that period. It is expressed as number of births per 1,000 population.
Urban area	An Urban area is characterized by higher population density and vast human features in comparison to areas surrounding it. Urban areas may be cities, towns or conurbations, but the term is not commonly extended to rural settlements such as villages and hamlets. Urban areas are created and further developed by the process of urbanization.
Suburbanization	Suburbanization (or suburbanisation) is a term used to describe the growth of areas on the fringes of major cities. It is one of the many causes of the increase in urban sprawl. Many residents of metropolitan areas no longer live and work within the central urban area, choosing instead to live in satellite communities called suburbs and commute to work via automobile or mass transit.
Zoning	Zoning is a device of land use regulation used by local governments in most developed countries . Zoning, or it may regulate building height, lot coverage, and similar characteristics, or some combination of these.

Theoretically, the primary purpose of Zoning is to segregate uses that are thought to be incompatible.

Commuting

Commuting is regular travel between one`s place of residence and place of work or full time study. Institutions that have few dormitories or near-campus student housing are called commuter schools in the United States.

Before the 19th century most workers lived less than an hour`s walk from their work.

Smart growth

Smart growth is an urban planning and transportation theory that concentrates growth in the center of a city to avoid urban sprawl; and advocates compact, transit-oriented, walkable, bicycle-friendly land use, including neighborhood schools, complete streets, and mixed-use development with a range of housing choices.

Smart growth values long-range, regional considerations of sustainability over a short-term focus. Its goals are to achieve a unique sense of community and place; expand the range of transportation, employment, and housing choices; equitably distribute the costs and benefits of development; preserve and enhance natural and cultural resources; and promote public health.

Air pollution	Air pollution is the introduction of chemicals, particulate matter, or biological materials that cause harm or discomfort to humans or other living organisms, or damages the natural environment, into the atmosphere. The atmosphere is a complex, dynamic natural gaseous system that is essential to support life on planet Earth. Stratospheric ozone depletion due to Air pollution has long been recognized as a threat to human health as well as to the Earth's ecosystems.
World Heritage Site	A UNESCO World Heritage Site is a site (such as a forest, mountain, lake, desert, monument, building, complex) that is on the list that is maintained by the international World Heritage Programme administered by the UNESCO World Heritage Committee, composed of 21 state parties which are elected by their General Assembly for a four-year term. A World Heritage Site is a place of either cultural or physical significance. The program catalogues, names, and conserves sites of outstanding cultural or natural importance to the common heritage of humanity.
Geothermal	The geothermal gradient is the rate at which the Earth's temperature increases with depth, indicating outward heat flows from a hot interior. Away from tectonic plate boundaries, it is 25-30° C per km of depth in most of the world. Strictly speaking, geo-thermal necessarily refers to the Earth but the concept may be applied to other planets.
Geothermal energy	Geothermal power is power extracted from heat stored in the earth. This Geothermal energy originates from the original formation of the planet, from radioactive decay of minerals, and from solar energy absorbed at the surface. It has been used for bathing since Paleolithic times and for space heating since ancient Roman times, but is now better known for generating electricity.
Birth rate	Crude Birth rate is the nativity or childbirths per 1,000 people per year. According to the United Nations' World Population Prospects: The 2008 Revision Population Database, crude Birth rate is the Number of births over a given period divided by the person-years lived by the population over that period. It is expressed as number of births per 1,000 population.
Bermuda Triangle	The Bermuda Triangle, also known as the Devil's Triangle, is a region in the western part of the North Atlantic Ocean in which a number of aircraft and surface vessels are alleged to have mysteriously disappeared in a manner that cannot be explained by human error, piracy, equipment failure, a suspension of the laws of physics, or activity by extraterrestrial beings. A substantial body of documentation reveals, however, that a significant portion of the allegedly mysterious incidents have been inaccurately reported or embellished by later authors, and numerous official agencies have stated that the number and nature of disappearances in the region is similar to any other area of ocean.

Natural gas	Natural gas is a gas consisting primarily of methane. It is found associated with other fossil fuels, in coal beds, as methane clathrates, and is created by methanogenic organisms in marshes, bogs, and landfills. It is an important fuel source, a major feedstock for fertilizers, and a potent greenhouse gas.
Middle East	The Middle East is a region that encompasses southwestern Asia and Egypt. In some contexts, the term has recently been expanded in usage to sometimes include Pakistan and Afghanistan, the Caucacus, and North Africa. It`s often used as a synonym for Near East, in opposition to Far East. The corresponding adjective is Middle-Eastern and the derived noun is Middle-Easterner.
Oil reserves	Oil reserves are the estimated quantities of crude oil that are claimed to be recoverable under existing economic and operating conditions.
	The total estimated amount of oil in an oil reservoir, including both producible and non-producible oil, is called oil in place. However, because of reservoir characteristics and limitations in petroleum extraction technologies, only a fraction of this oil can be brought to the surface, and it is only this producible fraction that is considered to be reserves.
Erosion	Erosion is a gravity driven process that moves solids (sediment, soil, rock and other particles) in the natural environment or their source and deposits them elsewhere. It usually occurs due to transport by wind, water, or ice; by down-slope creep of soil and other material under the force of gravity; or by living organisms, such as burrowing animals, in the case of bioerosion.
	erosion is a natural process, but it has been increased dramatically by human land use, especially industrial agriculture, deforestation, and urban sprawl.
Global warming	Global warming is the increase in the average temperature of Earth`s near-surface air and oceans since the mid-20th century and its projected continuation. Global surface temperature increased 0.74 ± 0.18 °C (1.33 ± 0.32 °F) between the start and the end of the 20th century. The Intergovernmental Panel on Climate Change (IPCC) concludes that most of the observed temperature increase since the middle of the 20th century was caused by increasing concentrations of greenhouse gases resulting from human activity such as fossil fuel burning and deforestation.
Ozone depletion	Ozone depletion describes two distinct, but related observations: a slow, steady decline of about 4% per decade in the total volume of ozone in Earth`s stratosphere (ozone layer) since the late 1970s, and a much larger, but seasonal, decrease in stratospheric ozone over Earth`s polar regions during the same period. The latter phenomenon is commonly referred to as the ozone hole. In addition to this well-known stratospheric ozone depletion, there are also tropospheric ozone depletion events, which occur near the surface in polar regions during spring.

Disease	A Disease or medical condition is an abnormal condition of an organism that impairs bodily functions, associated with specific symptoms and signs. It may be caused by external factors, such as infectious Disease, or it may be caused by internal dysfunctions, such as autoimmune Diseases. A cure is the end of a medical condition or a treatment that is very likely to end it, while remission refers to the disappearance, possibly temporarily, of symptoms.
Africa	Africa is the world`s second-largest and second most-populous continent, after Asia. At about 30.2 million km$^2$ (11.7 million sq mi) including adjacent islands, it covers 6% of the Earth`s total surface area and 20.4% of the total land area. With a billion people in 61 territories, it accounts for about 14.72% of the World`s human population.
Aral Sea	The Aral Sea is an endorheic basin in Central Asia; it lies between Kazakhstan (Aktobe and Kyzylorda provinces) in the north and Karakalpakstan, an autonomous region of Uzbekistan, in the south. The name roughly translates as `Sea of Islands`, referring to more than 1,500 islands that once dotted its waters. The maximum depth of the sea is 102 feet (31 m).
Genocide	Genocide is the deliberate and systematic destruction, in whole or in part, of an ethnic, racial, religious, a legal definition is found in the 1948 United Nations Convention on the Prevention and Punishment of the Crime of Genocide (CPPCG` The preamble to the CPPCG states that instances of Genocide have taken place throughout history, but it was not until Raphael Lemkin coined the term and the prosecution of perpetrators of the Holocaust at the Nuremberg trials that the United Nations agreed to the CPPCG which defined the crime of Genocide under international law.
Dam	A Dam is a barrier that impounds water or underground streams. Dams generally serve the primary purpose of retaining water, while other structures such as floodgates or levees (also known as dikes) are used to manage or prevent water flow into specific land regions. Hydropower and pumped-storage hydroelectricity are often used in conjunction with Dams to provide clean electricity for millions of consumers.
Sustainable development	Sustainable development is a pattern of resource use that aims to meet human needs while preserving the environment so that these needs can be met not only in the present, but also for future generations. The term was used by the Brundtland Commission which coined what has become the most often-quoted definition of Sustainable development(UNESCO, 2001) further elaborates the concept by stating that `...cultural diversity is as necessary for humankind as biodiversity is for nature`; it becomes `one of the roots of development understood not simply in terms of economic growth, but also as a means to achieve a more satisfactory intellectual, emotional, moral and spiritual existence`. In this vision, cultural diversity is the fourth policy area of Sustainable development.

CPSIA information can be obtained at www.ICGtesting.com
Printed in the USA
243661LV00001BA/133/P